JESUS HYPOTHESES

JESUS HYPOTHESES

V. MESSORI

Introduction by Malcolm Muggeridge

St Paul Publications

Original title: *Ipotesi su Gesù*,
Società Editrice Internazionale, Turin, 1976

English translation and adaptation
by Mary Smith

St Paul Publications
Slough SL3 6BT England

ISBN 085439 154 1 (Paper)
ISBN 085439 155 X (Cased)

Printed in Great Britain by offset lithography by
Billing & Sons Ltd, Guildford, London and Worcester

Dedicated to Blaise Pascal

Translator's note:

The English of the biblical quotations follows closely the Italian version used by the author, that of the *Bibbia Concordata*, Milan, 1968 (prepared for the Società Biblica Italiana by an inter-confessional committee and given official approval by Jews – O.T. only – and Catholics, Orthodox and Reformed denominations).

Contents

Introduction

One of the many marvels of the Gospels is that any honest and lively mind, exploring their account of the birth, ministry, death and resurrection of Jesus, is likely to come up with something fresh and wonderful in the process. This applies even to theologians, whose minds are not always honest and seldom lively. An Italian journalist, Vittorio Messori, is a case in point. He tackles the subject without any strong pre-suppositions or burdensome apparatus of scholarship; taking as his mentor none of the Fathers, not even Thomas Aquinas, but Blaise Pascal, a man of the Enlightenment, whose splendid intelligence and luminous words produced in his *Pensées* the greatest apologia for the Christian faith since Augustine's *City of God.* As I have found myself, there is no better guide than Pascal for a twentieth-century mind and disposition. His immense realism, his engrained scepticism and the beautiful faith that breaks through it, like a rainbow across a dark sky, his audacious resolution of Man's prospects in eternity to a wager on God's existence, which, as he points out, "if you win, you win everything; if you lose, you lose nothing" – all this speaks to us today with special force and poignancy, more especially in the light of Pascal's eminence as a scientist and a thinker. How fortunate, too, that Pascal left behind him only the notes for the extensive treatise he planned! Had he completed the work, it might well have proved recondite and tedious; whereas the notes, so terse and sparkling, form a bright and inexhaustibly interesting galaxy. Nietzsche saw Pascal as the "broken Christian", but after all it was Nietzsche who broke and went mad, whereas Pascal's death-mask, a cast of which I keep in my work-room, conveys a sanity and serenity as immaculate as his prose.

Like Vittorio Messori, then, I hold Pascal in great esteem. We have another point in common; we are both journalists, and so instinctively see the Gospels as copy rather than as texts. The distinction is very real, copy being something that you work on and over so that the words may impinge on a reader to the maximum degree, whereas a text is a subject for analysis, interpretation and speculation. To a journalist, it is ludicrous to suppose that the Gospels were faked to support the notion that Jesus was the promised Messiah when a couple of evenings' work by a competent sub-editor would have sufficed to eliminate all the contradictions, obscurities, anachronisms and general shaky historicity that theologians and form critics have been mulling over for centuries. In journalistic eyes, that is to say, the fact that the Gospels have such disparities is the guarantee of their authenticity; if they held together better they would be the less convincing.

So Vittorio Messori reasons, and I agree with him. His attitude reminds me of a story the dramatist, R.C. Sherriff, was fond of telling. He had been called to Hollywood to work on the film script of H.G. Well's story, *The Invisible Man*, some twenty previous attempts having proved unacceptable. Sherriff read through these abortive efforts, and felt quite incapable of producing anything likely to meet with more favour. Then, in desperation he turned to the story as originally written by Wells, and it seemed so good that, after making some minor adjustments, he decided to have it typed out and submitted as a proffered script. It was received with acclaim, and Sherriff's reputation as a brilliant adapter and script writer was established. In the same sort of way, Vittorio Messori has turned to the Gospels as they exist, and as through the centuries of Christendom they have been a source of edification and inspiration, and reached the conclusion that they are intrinsically true; that God did indeed intervene in history at a particular time and in the person of a particular Man; that, as it is so sublimely put in the Fourth Gospel, through the Incarnation the Word did veritably become flesh, to dwell among us full of grace and truth.

How otherwise could the Gospels have survived, to inspire over twenty centuries, as they have, such diverse minds and temperaments, to generate such a wealth of art and literature and music and architecture, to transform so many lives from devoting themselves to what Pascal calls "licking the earth" into dedicated service to their Creator and their fellow humans, seeing them all as brothers and sisters, members of one family, with, for father, a loving God? Vittorio Messori quotes Italo Zolli, sometime Chief Rabbi of the Jewish community in Rome, as saying after his conversion to Christianity: "The whole of the Old Testament appears to me like an enciphered telegram sent from God to men." The key for deciphering the telegram, he goes on, is Christ, in the light of whom "the thrill of expectancy that runs through all the books of the Old Testament takes on real meaning". In the New Testament the expectancy is over, and the realisation has come. Vittorio Messori's exposition of this realisation is warm-hearted, ingenious and persuasive, and if the conclusions he draws will not necessarily please or convince everyone – myself included – all must recognise the sincerity of his purpose and the worthwhileness of pursuing it.

Malcolm Muggeridge

1.

Supposing it's true . . . ?

Either God exists or he doesn't. Which alternative looks the better bet to you?
Neither. There's no sense in betting either way.
You are mistaken. You can't avoid choosing one or the other.

BLAISE PASCAL

In all the best circles Jesus-talk is barred.

Like death, money and sex, Jesus is a topic of conversation guaranteed to elicit stony stares if mentioned in any enlightened drawing-room.

There has been too much exaggerated popular piety down the centuries; too many sentimental portrayals of 'gentle Jesus meek and mild', the fair-haired, blue-eyed wonder-boy dear to the hearts of Victorian mammas; too much sugary mush fed to children preparing for First Communion.

Small wonder that the name of Jesus rings sickly sweet in the ears of the 'élite'. For them, Jesus-talk is utterly taboo.

You can get a doctorate in history without so much as a glance at the problem posed by the life of that obscure Jewish carpenter who split history in two: *before* Christ and *after* Christ.

You can get a doctorate in classics – and know all about Graeco-Roman mythology after poring over the original texts – without ever attempting to tackle the Greek of the New Testament.

It's strange. The years came to a halt at Jesus, and then set off again from him. Yet he himself seems to have been hidden away.

Either he gets ignored altogether or else he is taken as read.

Even priests, bishops and popes say precious little about him. True enough, they do make passing allusions to him every Sunday, in innumerable sermons and homilies.

But all too often it seems as if, for them, belief in him presents no sort of problem. They all place wonderful constructions on the Gospel, but few of them venture below ground to check whether any foundations exist in the minds of their hearers. Few of them set out to test whether the corner-stone of their faith and their churches still holds firm today.

Jesus is the only man in the whole of human history to whom the name of God has been directly attributed. But a great many people have presumably become insensitive to this appalling scandal. They just take it for granted. As one flippant observer remarked: it's as if all the incense has befuddled them.

There is a 'secret' saying of Jesus in one of the apocryphal gospels: *"He who marvels will attain to the Kingdom."* A great many people seem to have lost the gift of marvel, the gift of wonder.

The newspapers, and secular publications in general, pay a certain amount of attention to the institutions that have grown up around the faith (the Vatican, the churches ...) but they ignore the faith itself. And the specifically Christian publications seem concerned principally with varieties of asceticism, or pious meditation on Jesus; they seldom face up to the immense historical problem he poses.

So it would seem that nobody tackles 'the Jesus problem'. But that is very far from true. There is a veritable sea of books about him, and a perpetually storm-tossed sea it is too.

For centuries now, discussion of Jesus has been the jealously guarded preserve of clerics and lay academics, themselves often ex-clerics. It is these specialists who have produced, and still do produce, those books by the thousand, endlessly confuting one another with learned disputations.

Ordinary people have to make do with little books of devotions or odds and ends of pop-theology, often all too bland when they are not blatantly propagandist in tone.

Consequently many people are quite unaware that every imaginable hypothesis about Jesus has already been suggested and rejected, defended and demolished, reformulated ... ad infinitum. And of all the texts in the world, the New Testament is the one that has received far and away the most meticulous analysis.

Little more than faint echoes of this debate ever reach the non-specialist, although it has now been going on for nearly two thousand years. Until the eighteenth century almost all the argument went on within Christianity itself, with 'orthodoxy' combating 'heresy'; but then came the waves of criticism from outside. The historicity of the Scriptures on which the faith is based began to be challenged. Attacks that were often bitterly and ruthlessly polemical were mounted against what had hitherto been unquestioned: belief in a specific relationship between God and the man Jesus, faith in Jesus as the Christ, the Messiah, the one who was to come to Israel.

But the arguments are still confined to a small number of initiates. Jean Guitton, the French scholar to whom this book owes a great deal, has written:

'The general public has come to the firm conclusion that "the Jesus problem" is far beyond its own competence – a matter for wise men and theologians only. Because of the difficulty of forming a personal opinion, unbelievers and believers alike refrain from thinking about it at all – the former so as to cosset their doubts about the historical veracity of the Jesus of the gospels, the latter so as to live by faith. So silence once again reigns over this fundamental problem.'

The author of the book you are now reading decided to defy the silence and poach on the specialists' preserve.

I am an outsider who has dared to venture into the inner sanctums where all is expressed in German or Latin and where battle is joined over Hebrew semantics, Aramaic inscriptions and Greek codices. I am neither an academic nor an ecclesiastic. I am a mere layman.

This book has arisen out of my journalist's urge to collect information – in the first place for myself – and then put it at the disposal of the reading public.

I am at home in the newsrooms of the dailies and the editorial offices of the weeklies, not in the lecture-rooms of the pontifical universities. Nor do I come from a Christian background.

My only reason for saying a little about myself – at risk of being a bore – is my wish to assure the reader that I began from a position of doubt; or rather of indifference. Like so many people nowadays. Definitely not from a position of faith. I embarked on this enquiry after eighteen years of state education; so everything had to be learned, starting from scratch.

The only priests I came across as a schoolboy were the ones who took the 'religion' classes stipulated by the Concordat.

Then, quite unexpectedly, my first-century-Palestine treasure-hunt began. First in the chain of clues was a copy of Pascal's *Pensées* which I bought in order to do some quite peripheral research for a Political Sciences doctorate.

This book is dedicated to Blaise Pascal because without him it would never have been written. Or it would have been completely different, anyway.

It is also dedicated to the host of people who through the centuries have sought the answer to the most intriguing of all detective stories: the origin of Christianity.

One does not have to be addicted to detective stories to be caught up in this one. The mere fact of being alive makes each one of us an interested party.

'Vous êtes embarqués', 'You are in it too', Pascal reminds anyone who tries to run away from the problem of his own destiny.

Whether we like it or not, the name 'Jesus' has for centuries – in Europe, America, Africa, Australasia and parts of Asia – been bound up with our understanding of our destiny.

Those who believe this name to be the definitive answer to all man's searchings, linking it directly with the extraordinary concept 'Son of God' and affirming that each one of us is drawn into its history, still continue stubbornly to proclaim it – as they have ever since the days of the Roman empire.

In this book I have tried to examine the justification for a certain obscure Palestinian's claim to be the 'Saviour' of mankind.

I shall try to explain why, for me, he alone of all the religious leaders the world has known is worth getting to know. Why Jesus, and not Mohammed or Lao-Tse or Zarathrustra.

I have compiled a dossier of information providing answers to my own questions – to some of them at least, though certainly not to all. They are questions that I hope are asked by ordinary men and women, people for whom every day brings its problems. Problems often so intense and intractable that there is no time left for seeking solutions to *the* Problem, the fundamental one and the overriding one.

I mean the Problem that underlies questions – often derided as 'adolescent stuff unworthy of an adult' – such as 'Who are we?', 'Where have we come from?', 'Where are we going?'

Is there a future for us on the far side of an indeterminate horizon? Or are we simply merchandise wrapped up by the midwife and sent on its way to the undertaker?

At both ends of life there is mystery. Before birth and

after death our existence is plunged in the unknown. In eternity, no doubt.

The human condition has been likened to that of someone who wakes to find himself unaccountably on some train speeding through the night. Where did it start from, this train we have been bundled onto without knowing when or why? Where is it heading for? And why this particular train and not some other one?

Some people are perfectly content to examine their compartment, calculate the size of the seats and discover what everything is made of. Then they quietly drop off to sleep again. Having familiarised themselves with their environment they ask no more questions; anything else is 'none of their business'. After all, if fear of the unknown does at times catch hold of one, it can always be shaken off by thinking of something else.

'I do not know who put me into the world, nor what the world is, nor what I am myself. I see the terrifying spaces of the universe hemming me in, and I find myself attached to one corner of this vast expanse without knowing why I have been put in this place rather than that, or why the brief span of life allotted to me should be assigned to one moment rather than another of all the eternity which went before me and all that which will come after me. I see only infinity on every side, hemming me in like an atom or like the shadow of a fleeting instant. All I know is that I must soon die, but what I know least about is this very death which I cannot evade.'

'Sublime but mad', 'sick and unbalanced', 'incurably childish', 'a conceited ass who thought he could get the better of the law of doubt', 'a genius stolen from science': those are just some of the labels that have been slapped on Pascal who wrote those lines. He was in fact guilty of having spent his life enquiring whether there might perhaps be some solution to the mystery of the human condition.

Foreseeing the ironic comments of his deathbed well-wishers, he played the ironist himself: 'In order to be happy the human race, having failed to find a cure for death, has decided not to give it a thought.'

Or, with a tinge of bitterness: 'Man's sensitivity to small matters and his insensitivity to great matters are indicative of extraordinary perversity.'

But in point of fact Pascal had equal love and esteem for both the believer and the unbeliever – for anyone willing to stake all in the gamble of living. 'Either God exists or he doesn't. On which alternative are you going to place your bet?'

However, he was at a loss to understand the attitude of anyone who declined to commit himself one way or the other: 'Suppose an heir comes across the papers establishing his lineage. Do you think he will say "They may be false" and make no attempt to check them?' And then, with that provocative bluntness of his which offends the squeamish but which others find appealing: 'That God exists is proved not only by the zealous devotion of those who seek him but also by the indifference of those who don't.'

Going back to the idea of the train, here even the know-alls can say only one thing for certain: that in the end it will enter a dark tunnel before anybody has been able to get off it. But what there may be beyond the entrance to the mysterious tunnel they do not know.

Some say: 'There's nothing; only darkness.'

That is a perfectly respectable opinion, but it suffers from the defect of being unproven. Nobody has come back again to tell us of his travels on the far side of the grave.

Others of us are not ashamed to admit to being dismayed by the eternal silence of the infinite spaces around us. Instead of staying placidly in our seats and letting the darkness rush by outside, we move about from compartment to compartment – in the hope of finding some sort of timetable that will give a name and a destination to this journey that is not of our own choosing.

So besides answering some questions I have tried to impart some information. I have collected a number of relevant items in an attempt to set out a 'for and against' working hypothesis, albeit a modest one, concerning the 'Jesus problem'.

He is the one and only man in history of whom it is said that he came back alive out of death's tunnel.

Supposing it's true?

More than ten years ago I set about making, in typical journalist fashion, an investigation that I hoped would provide an anwer to that question; and I ended up completely enthralled by it. Perhaps Pascal's Christ is right yet again: "You would not have sought me unless you had already found me."

The little I have to offer is nonetheless offered in all honesty. As I was looking into it all principally in my own interest, I naturally tried not to deceive myself. And God, if he exists, has no need of any lies concocted by us. The historical figure called Jesus, who for twenty centuries has been bound up with the idea of God, has a right to the plain truth and not ingenious apologetics. And we ourselves have the right to be fed not with tendentious propaganda but with straightforward information.

I have therefore tried to keep to what is, as far as possible, not in dispute.

After so many learned and meticulous analyses there seems to be a need for somebody very ordinary to risk attempting a synthesis. The one in this book is purely provisional – a simple suggestion that needs to be checked and discussed, improved on and reformulated. Unfortunately any book – by its very nature – is an 'authoritarian' means of communication, or anyway a monologue; the Gospel, by contrast, is a never-ending dialogue: "*But you, who do you say I am?"* is the question still being asked by its enigmatic protagonist.

My debt to all who have concerned themselves with the problem, no matter what their conclusions, is so great that I can say with Pascal: 'Authors who refer to their work as "my book", "my commentary", "my history" are like men of property who are forever talking about "my estates". They would do better to say "our book", "our commentary", "our history", since there is usually more owed to others than to themselves in what they have written.'

Frankly, to each and every sentence I could have appended a footnote giving a reference to someone else's work; but I have chosen to go to the opposite extreme and provide almost no footnotes at all.

As a matter of fact the scholars are not going to read this book which owes so much to their painstaking researches. Many of them will pour scorn on it as an act of trespass on the part of an inquisitive amateur – a gate-crasher who has had the bad taste to drag into the open a dispute far too subtle for the general public to understand.

In any case, in the unlikely event of the book finding any specialist readers, its lack of notes will cause them no inconvenience: they know perfectly well where to check the statements I have borrowed if they want to. Its other readers, 'outsiders' like myself, can rest assured that what I quote is quoted accurately, without any tendentious twists, and that every bit of information has been and can be documented.

I have done my best to overcome the natural diffidence one is bound to feel when, as is the case with me, one is still a seeker after the truth. Paul of Tarsus described his state of mind on appearing at Corinth as *'weak, in fear and trembling'*. If I may be allowed to liken myself, at least in the matter of weakness, to that astonishing PR man for early Christianity, let me say that my own state of mind is identical with his. But I have also felt in duty bound to respond to the call of another Jew, Simon called Peter: *'Always be ready to account for the hope that is in you when anybody asks you for an explanation of it. But do so with courtesy and respect.'*

'Courtesy and respect.'

In tackling this problem of Jesus, who meets man head-on as well as overtaking him from behind, everybody's contribution is needed. So to engage in polemics is worse than useless: it is plain stupid.

I have every sympathy with the so-called 'sceptics' who wish that Christians would stop being credulous; indeed, credulity is far from equivalent to belief. Were it not for the 'sceptics' we would still be at the stage of baroque apologetics in this matter.

Lacordaire, the disciple of Voltaire who ended up as a Dominican, wrote: 'What matters to me is not to prove those who disagree with me to be wrong-headed, but rather to attain to a higher truth together with them.'

So far, it appears to me that – in spite of everything – nothing about Jesus fails to add up; that the final step for a reasonable human being to take is to acknowledge the existence of a dimension that transcends reason itself; and that it is perfectly reasonable to stake everything on that hypothesis.

Much mystery of course remains unprobed, with barely a ray of light to pierce it, and innumerable specific problems remain unsolved. If the Creator of the universe did indeed enter time and space, why did he choose this tiny fragment of rock and metal orbiting round one star among the thousands in our galaxy alone?

'To believe is not to understand everything', said Teilhard de Chardin. However, that mystery and those problems seem to me even greater if one opts for the opposite solution. That is to say, if one asserts that Christianity is nothing but the crassest misunderstanding the human race has fallen prey to.

Moreover, 'why should anyone condemn Christians for being unable to give rational grounds for their belief, since they openly profess that it is folly, *stultitia ?'* (Pascal).

Paul of Tarsus in fact did class as 'folly' the message that God himself had appeared in the shape of a penniless Jewish craftsman, and that this same 'failure' of a man had conquered death by rolling back the stone that sealed his tomb. Folly it certainly was to the worldly-wise.

'When he mentioned rising from the dead, some of them (the Athenians) *burst out laughing; others said: "We would like to hear you talk about this another time." After that Paul left them'* (Acts, chapter 17).

On the very morning of that rising from the dead, the account of it attributed to Luke states that *'two men in shining garments'* appeared to the women who had come to the tomb.

"Why look among the dead for someone who is alive?", the two men asked.

This question recorded in the Gospel might aptly be applied to all investigation of the Jesus of history, the man whom people knew nearly two thousand years ago.

All the same, if one is ever to acknowledge that every man, then and now, is the Christ of faith, one cannot avoid starting from the Jesus who was born under Augustus and died under Tiberius.

Similarly if one is to maintain that wherever men engage in struggle on behalf of mankind, the God of Abraham and of Jesus manifests himself yet again in history. And that wherever people strive for justice, and for deliverance from all that oppresses man both outwardly and inwardly, there is to be found the People of God, the *ecclesia*, the assembly of all who believe in the risen Jesus – whether or not they know his name.

2.

A hidden God, and a disconcerting one . . .

> *Before they attack this religion, let them at least learn what it is. If this religion were to boast that it had clear sight of God, and plain and manifest evidence of his existence, one could effectively raise the objection that there is nothing discernible in the world to demonstrate it conclusively. But since, on the contrary, Christianity says that men are in darkness and remote from God, that he has hidden himself from their understanding, that this is the very name he gives himself in scripture: the hidden God* (Deus absconditus) ...
>
> BLAISE PASCAL

Science is not enough

God, if there is a God, is hidden.

If he does indeed exist, it is plain fact that men have always needed to feel their way towards him. And men's gropings have not always brought them certainty one way or the other. People who declare that belief comes easily to them are quite astonishing; perhaps they haven't fully understood what believing really entails.

The human race has found from bitter experience that no deity is to be seen peeping out from behind the clouds. Heaven and earth both remain silent.

But, if God does indeed exist, it is not only the silence of nature that hides him. He is concealed by the reality of innocent victims' sufferings, sufferings that seem to indict him unanswerably. He is also concealed by the multiplicity of the religions; and within those religions by the obscurity of so many of the 'sacred writings', the Bible included; by the shortcomings of the churches, the errors and inconsistencies of the very people who ought to be testifying to his existence by the lives they lead.

'Why so, Lord? Here you see men, your own creation, stricken and despairing, crying out for help; if you do indeed exist, all you need do to bring them running towards you is let them glimpse the light of your eyes, the hem of your raiment; and yet you refrain?' (Teilhard de Chardin).

In the search for God that goes on generation after generation, no decisive help is provided by either science or philosophy – at least for the greater part of humanity.

Pascal remarked, apropos believers for whom faith in God presents no problems: 'I am amazed by the rashness with which these people set about talking about God. They address their arguments to sceptics and they always begin by proving the existence of the deity by way of the works of nature'; but 'to go about it like that is to provide the sceptics with evidence for believing the reasons adduced by Christians to be very defective. Both my reason and my experience convince me that nothing is more likely to inspire in them disdain for religion.'

Suppose we look at his own dialogue, in the *Pensées*, between a sceptic and a believer:

The sceptic: "Come now, surely you are going to say that the sky and the birds prove the existence of God?"

The believer: "No."

The sceptic: "But isn't that what your religion says?"

The believer: "No. Because although it is true of a few who are endowed with special intuition, it is not true of the majority of people."

And it is often false for the minority too, even for humanity's élites. For it is perfectly possible to win a Nobel prize for astronomy or physics, to be an outstanding professor of zoology, to know all about botany or biology, the amazing social structures of the insect world or the incredible complexity of the human brain – all that and much more – and still be *either* an atheist *or* a believer.

Down-to-earth experience has shown that the world of nature is not necessarily a launching-pad towards God. Conversely, in spite of the exaggerated claims of old-time materialism, the natural sciences do not eliminate God from the world. The history of human thought to date has shown that natural science is often powerless to resolve the eternal conflict between faith and disbelief.

Philosophical 'proofs' of God

Philosophy too has shown itself capable of being, for some, the way to God. But for others it has been the way to atheism; and for others still to agnosticism, to "we don't know and we never shall know".

So it is strange that Christian thought should have seen fit to formulate for itself certain philosophical 'proofs' to 'demonstrate' that God exists.

By so doing Christians themselves – those who maintain that God is a reality, an actual man to be found in history – are in danger of reducing God to an object for speculation, one on which to set to work with scientific and philosophical discussion techniques. Instead of being the *subject* whose call one is ready to answer in the course of each day that dawns, God is in danger of being reduced to an *object* to be caged behind the bars of natural theology, like a wild animal in a zoo.

This reduces even Christianity – the only religious message in human history to be based not on some wise insight but on a precise historical assertion ("I believe that the man Jesus, who died under Pontius Pilate, rose from the dead at Jerusalem") – to the level of a philosophy little different from any other. Mere abstraction.

Believers ought surely to find this disturbing.

For those who are not believers – to quote Pascal once more since he cannot be bettered: 'These philosophical proofs of God are so complex, and so remote from the way ordinary people think, that they make little or no impression. Even if some people were to find them useful, it would be for the time being only, while they were following the argument. An hour later they would suspect they had been deceived.'

These 'proofs' confirm belief rather than produce it; they are an attempt on the part of believers to allow reason a share in the certainty of faith.

Moreover, it is not only the suitability and practical effectiveness of these 'proofs' that are open to question. For some time now their validity too has been disputed. The thinking that devised them rested on the logic of classical philosophy, Aristotle for the most part. Nowadays a great many thinkers reject that type of logic; or at least they deny that it is the only possible way of reasoning.

At the first Vatican Council in 1870, the Catholic Church declared that it is *possible* to solve the problem of God by scientific and philosophical reasoning.

But it has never asserted that all men, in actual fact, succeed in doing so.[1]

Nor does it say that the God disclosed by natural science and philosophy is invariably the God who came 'not to be served but to serve' mankind. The theoretical concept of the 'existence of the divine' is by no means necessarily a value to which it is worth committing oneself for life.

What conceivable difference can it make, to a human being with a need to love and be loved, to arrive at admitting the possibility of a hidden Static Motive Force regulating the universe? Or an impersonal principle of Being responsible for the working of the digestive processes?

Here is Pascal again, the man whose genius in physics and mathematics had made the whole of Europe gasp:

'If somebody were to become convinced that the properties of the numerals are eternal abstract truths deriving from and dependent on a primordial truth in which they subsist and which is called "God", it would not seem to me that this conviction brought that person very far along the way of salvation.'

That is why he declared that 'the sky and the birds are no proof of God' – not the God of the Christians anyway – and that, ultimately, 'the whole of philosophy is not worth a single hour's study'.

Man in the real, no stranger to either laughter or tears, stands in need not of brain-taxing disputation but of a message that will warm his heart, allay his fears and give meaning to his life.

The God of the philosophers and scientists can provide none of what man yearns for. Provable or not, he is not a value that whets our appetites.

But besides being uncertain and useless, he is also dangerous – as we shall try to show later.

Only for Jews and Christians is God a hidden God

So God, if he does indeed exist, is hidden; and neither natural science nor philosophy is an instrument capable of guiding all men towards the mystery of the divine.

The outward appearance of this world of ours provides no evidence of either the total absence or the obvious presence of a deity. Rather the evidence suggests a God who conceals his presence. A God whom man cannot reach except by way of a free gift, a revelation.

Pascal drew from this an uncompromising conclusion: 'Since God, if he does indeed exist, is hidden, any religion that does not assert that God is hidden cannot be true.' He goes on to argue that if this is indeed the principle by which to assess a religion's veracity, only Christianity can be 'true'.

In point of fact only Christianity includes among its fundamental beliefs the statement that God withdrew from the sight of men. In this it draws on the great and revered Hebrew tradition out of which it sprang.

Judeo-Christianity's faith is rooted in history, which is

seen as the terrain where God and man go in search of one another and find one another.

There is no point in going in search of the obvious.

Moreover, only in the Judeo-Christian tradition does one find 'apologetics' – that branch of theology that is principally concerned with 'demonstrating' the existence of God. Leaving aside any judgment as to its effectiveness, the methods adopted by Hebrew and Christian apologetics do indicate that the God of Abraham, Isaac, Jacob and Jesus has to be sought after and found, and that there is a need for this God to be 'demonstrated'.

Does one really go to the trouble of demonstrating what is self-evident?

In the Old Testament the God of the Jews, Yahweh, said: *"I dwell in thick darkness"* (1 Kings, chapter 8).

When Moses asked to be allowed to *'see his glory'*, Yahweh replied: *"You cannot see my face, for man cannot see me and remain alive."* Even the 'founder' of the Jewish faith was allowed to see only God's back: *"You shall see my back; but my face shall not be seen"* (Exodus, chapter 33).

"Truly you are a hidden God, the God of Israel, the Saviour", says the prophet Isaiah (chapter 45) in a passage dear to Pascal.

So in the Judaic tradition Yahweh is a God who hides himself away; he certainly seeks us, but we for our part have also to seek him. In this, as in many other respects, he differs profoundly from the God of every other religion.

From time to time the difference was in danger of being attenuated by the infiltration of ideas foreign to the Hebrew view. Take for instance the beginning of chapter 13 of the book of Wisdom, the work of a hellenised Jew: *'Yes, naturally stupid are all men who have not known God and who, from the good things that can be seen, have not been able to know Him-who-is, or, while studying the works, have failed to recognise their Artificer.'* Yahweh, the hidden God who dwells in the thick darkness, would seem here to be put on a par with the gods of the Greek philosophies. But the mind and culture of Judaism reacted adversely to this 'pollution', and the book of Wisdom is excluded from the canon of the Jewish Bible. For the Jews, God was to be sought not in nature but in history. But in history there is room for misunderstanding as well as certainty.

Christianity has inherited and fully accepted this disturbing lack of evidence for God's existence. Not only is the reality of the *Deus absconditus*, the God who hides himself, accepted: it is considered by the Christian scriptures to be part and parcel of the relationship between man and God. In the Hebrew tradition it was often no more than sensed by intuition and sketchily expressed, but in Christianity it is fully developed.

"Righteous Father, the world has not known you", says Jesus in the seventeenth chapter of John's gospel, in the solemn prayer before the Passion.

And at the beginning of his gospel the same writer states that *'Nobody has ever seen God; it is the only Son, who is nearest to the Father's heart, who has made him known.'*

The Jesus of Matthew's gospel exclaims: *"I bless you, Father, Lord of heaven and earth, for hiding these things from the learned and the clever and revealing them to mere children."* And *"no one knows the Father except the Son and those to whom the Son chooses to reveal him"* (chapter 11).

This idea of the hiddenness of God, so repugnant to alien religions, was often stressed by the apostles, Paul in particular. God wished, he said in Athens, that men *'should seek him and, by feeling their way towards him, find him. Yet he is not far from any of us'* (Acts 17).

And in his letter to the Corinthians, chapter 1: *'the world did not know God through wisdom'.* Later in that letter (chapter 13) Paul wrote that during their earthly life men are able to discern only vaguely what is hidden in the 'thick darkness' the early scriptures spoke of: *'Now we see only a blurred image, as if in a rough mirror.'* Only after death, he asserts, shall we see *'face to face'*.

The early Fathers of the Church laid heavy stress on this idea. 'Knowledge of God comes to us through shadows and enigmas', wrote St Cyril, Patriarch of Alexandria.

As the centuries progressed, mysticism was to assert that the 'art of being saints' – that is to say of being Christian through and through – consists in one thing only: believing in spite of everything. In spite of all that appears to contradict belief, all that seems to negate human hope and human expectation.

An understandably discreet reserve

Christianity is thus the only religion to take into full account the fact that God's nature, and even his existence, constitute a problem for mankind. Not only that: in a development of the Hebrew insight it goes so far as to make this 'hiddenness' an indispensable element of its belief.

If one reflects upon this 'hiddenness' (which is accepted only in the Judeo-Christian tradition) one can discern certain reasons for it. 'If there were no darkness, man would not be aware of his own wretchedness; if there were no light, he would not hope for salvation.' Moreover, 'faith is such a splendid thing that it is only right that those who cannot take the trouble to seek it should be deprived of it'. So, 'there is light enough for those who want to believe, and darkness enough for those who do not' (Pascal).

It would seem as if God does not wish to 'save' man without man's consent.

Simone Weil, a Jewess with an agnostic upbringing, has given an answer from a rationalist angle to the instinctive and recurrent protests men make about the lack of evidence for God's existence. 'Perhaps God has allowed us to perceive only as much of himself as will inspire men, through faith in him, to care for one another. Enough for man not to be so fascinated by heaven that he loses interest in this earth.'

Nobody loves more deeply, she goes on to say, than someone who respects the freedom of others. The discreet reserve of God, who does not thunder majestically from the heavens, seems like a salute to human freedom, the greatest of all safeguards for man's liberty to choose for himself what his destiny shall be. Only a hidden God can establish with man a relationship of freedom, not one of need.

This acceptance of the hiddenness of God can be shown to contain unsuspected depths of meaning. Jean Guitton has written: 'For Christians, God is of necessity discreet. He has given a semblance of probability to the doubts surrounding his existence. He has veiled himself with shadow so as to make our faith more ardent and also, no doubt, so as to preserve his right to forgive us when we deny him. The answer that rejects belief needs to retain a degree of verisimilitude if God's mercy is to operate in total freedom.'

The God of Abraham and Jesus: a God to be met

For the writers of the Hebrew and Christian scriptures there is another reason why God's presence cannot be anything but discreet. From this one reason all the others derive.

For the scripture writers, God is a Person in the fullest and most absolute sense of the word. He is a Person who sets out in search of persons, of mankind. *The* Person par excellence; and yet discoverable and knowable like any other person.

Let us consider our down-to-earth experience.

When is it possible for me to declare that I really know another person, that there has been a real meeting of minds between us? When the other person lets me know his inner thoughts and feelings, and when I accept in good faith what he discloses to me of himself. Every real meeting of minds presupposes on the one hand self-disclosure and on the other hand trust, belief, faith. What is true of our human encounters is true also of the encounter between God and man.

This is why, for the Christian, knowing God entails far more than simply affirming that he exists. That road is the one leading to the God of other religions – to the God of Islam, for instance, whose true nature is shown by the names used: *islam* means 'submission', and the *Muslim* is 'the one who submits'. That is a God who cannot be called Father.

Nor, in order to know God, is it enough – for the Christian – to accumulate proofs. That road is the one leading to the God of a number of philosophers and scientists – a God who can be acknowledged to exist, but a God lacking real value for us humans. Not only that, but a God who is wide open to the two fundamental objections raised by modern thought, i.e. that science manages perfectly well without him, and that the evil which has always distorted this world is an indictment of him. This is the God of deism (which in Pascal's view is as far removed from Christianity as atheism) – a God who has nothing in common with the God of Abraham and Jesus. Such is in fact the case, even though believers have all too often sorely misunderstood and thought that the two ideas of God, the biblical one of the Hebrew and Christian revelation and the philosophical one of 'the wisdom of this world', could be one and the same.

Some attempt to sort out the confusion seems essential.

"If you knew me, you would know the Father too"

It is a long story and a sad one. Here it can only be briefly sketched.

The Jesus of scripture revealed an image of God quite different from the image of him reached by philosophy and the other religions. All these construct a concept of a deity whose basic attributes are *existence* and *omnipotence*. But

Jesus revealed a God whose primary attribute is *love.* A God who caused Peter, awestruck by the Messiah who performed the duty of a servant, to cry out: "*You shall never wash my feet!*" (John 13). A concept of a deity embodied not in a king but in a slave, the humblest of all household slaves, the one detailed to wash the master's feet.

And it is this Jesus, portrayed in the gospels as God, who is said to have declared that only by looking to him – and not by trusting human philosophisings – can men reach some understanding of the nature of God.

"*If you knew me, you would know my Father too*"; "*Whoever sees me sees the one who sent me*"; so Jesus affirms, according to the gospel of John (chapters 8 and 12).

But as a result of much theologising, the God whom Jesus made known, the God who is a servant because he is love, got laced into the strait-jacket of 'natural theology' – the theology that is dependent on religious and philosophical speculation; precisely the sort of theology that Jesus had forbidden men to engage in. Addressing the Father he had said, according to the gospels: "*The world has not known you.*" Yet Plato's 'God the Idea' and Aristotle's 'God the Prime Mover', the Gods conjectured by men, gradually came to be identified with the God revealed by scripture. The Greek philosophers, refined, methodical and 'humane', were called upon to introduce 'culture' to the 'uncouth' gospels that so offend commonsense.

Almost as if to disguise even more successfully this God who is 'too unconventional', there was an attempt in the Middle Ages to enlist the aid of Islamic philosophy, of Mohammed's wise men. That has led some people to forget the extraordinary originality of the gospel message and assert that monotheism is the shared base of religions that, while differing from one another in dogma, rites and nomenclature, are substantially equal to one another. For don't they all proclaim belief in one single God?

All this was the reverse of what Christ had prescribed: instead of starting from him in order to reach some understanding of God, people started from human ideas of 'God' in order to 'explain' the God of Christ. The mantle of philosophy, Greek, Roman or Islamic, got thrown – as if in prudery or fear – over the bare shoulders of Jesus.

The Christian, who was meant to understand the nature of God not by way of abstruse metaphysical speculation but by looking to the teaching and behaviour of his Master, thus finds himself dragged into the doubtful company of those who have put together for themselves a God in their own image and likeness. From being a *subject* to be met and known, God becomes an *object* to be constructed on the basis of a model.[2]

The salt of Christianity has lost its savour. It lost it on the road leading away from history (the history contained in one particular collection of Judeo-Christian writings – 'salvation history') and towards philosophy; towards those theoretical constructions which, though admirable in themselves, have little or nothing to do with the Christian revelation.

Why revelation, if Aristotle and the other wise men had provided adequate answers to men's questions?

'Eloquent wisdom' does indeed, as Paul feared in his first letter to the Corinthians, *'empty the cross of Christ of its power'*. Omnipotence becomes the model, power the ideal.

Trying to interpret the records

Getting to know God can call for little more than setting out in search of him in a trustful frame of mind – on the supposition that he revealed at least something of himself in Jesus of Nazareth.

That is what faith claims *did* happen.

We shall therefore try to discern the meaning of what has been recorded about this man of flesh and blood, the only one to whom mankind has ever attributed the name of God himself. The approach via history is the only one that will enable us to decipher something of the enigma constituted by the God of the Christians.

This is a God who – so faith asserts – is so much a part of history that he took upon himself the form of an obscure member of a subject race in a remote province of the Roman empire.

And yet it has been said that in Jesus God continued to remain hidden, woven into the texture of human history; more than ever hidden because he reveals himself in ways and places of his own choosing; never open to coercion or manipulation by man.

The prophet Isaiah put these words into the mouth of Yahweh, Israel's God: "*Your ways are not my ways. … The heavens are as high above the earth as my ways are above your ways, my thoughts above your thoughts*" (chapter 55).

Just as that God eludes all attempts on the part of human wisdom to dispel the mystery that surrounds him, so the unpretentious and veiled manifestation of him that faith sees in Jesus eludes all the brash approaches of historians who try to expose him to the powerful spotlights of modern scientific methodology.

Any historian tackling the problem will always come up against a mystery: the ups and downs of research into Jesus have proved this to be the case. It is this mystery that explains the diffident approach of the evangelists and the first-century theologians; it has never been definitively explained by either historians or theologians, and it never will be. No biographer can ever do more than record the data pertaining to the mystery. He can advance hypotheses, but he cannot induce faith; for this is something enigmatic, beyond the capability of any man – be he philosopher, historian or what you will – to induce.

The God of the Bible, the God who is said to have spoken to Abraham and manifested himself in Jesus, is the only God worth getting to know. We shall try to demonstrate that this is so. And we shall also try to explain the sense in which this is the only image of God that one can talk about without getting side-tracked into one cul-de-sac or another by modern habits of thought.

But let us repeat that the sole purpose of this book is to stimulate others to carry out their own investigations. Because, to quote Pascal yet again, "The reasons we discover ourselves are far more convincing than the ones we learn from others."

The accusation of 'fideism'

Let us again insist that Christianity is the only religious message that is based not on some 'wisdom' or 'idea' but on a series of historical assertions, one in particular: *I believe that Jesus rose from the dead.* Hebrew belief was similarly historical: *I believe that God has spoken to Israel through his prophets.*

So, although we say to the philosophers "Stick to the philosophies", we are surely in duty bound to confront the Judeo-Christian claim to historicity with the findings of the historians – when those findings are free of philosophical bias.

It has rightly been remarked that 'both undiscerning acceptance of the Gospel portrayal of Jesus and partial or total rejection of it are conclusions dictated by criteria that are more philosophical than historical'. Innumerable travesties of Christ have resulted from the undue influence exerted by one philosophy or another on study of the historical problem presented by the origins of Christianity. All these travesties have been coloured by whatever ideology happened to be fashionable at the time.

Christianity has to be examined according to the criteria of its own 'genre'. It is belief in certain events which are said to have taken place at a certain time and in a certain place. We shall therefore take what seems to be the most sensible approach to a problem of this kind: we shall try to discuss the most objective data there is – events that can be accepted by all without argument.

Admittedly, quite a number of Christians are suspicious of this type of approach which they class as 'fideism' – an irrational surrender to faith unsupported by reason. But the accusation of fideism is levelled by believers who tackle the problem of the one and only historical faith in human history with tools that are purely philosophical. Tools that would be of service to Muslims, Hindus, Buddhists, or followers of Confucius or Zoroaster, but which are quite inadequate in the case of the God proclaimed by Christians: 'Jesus is the Lord because, though crucified by Pilate, he rose again.'

If anything, the historical method this book is going to adopt towards the origins of Christianity might more justifiably be accused of rationalism – the exact opposite of fideism. For we are going to appeal to reason, and insist on the most rigorous application of reason in assessing the historical credibility of what is asserted by scripture, above all by the gospels.

Nevertheless, if we become convinced, having thus applied reason to the matter, that the documentation backing up the message can be relied upon, then we can only have recourse once again to Pascal: 'The final step for reason to take is to acknowledge that there are many, many things beyond reason's reach.' (Or even to Shakespeare's Hamlet: 'There are more things in heaven and earth, Horatio, than are dreamed of in your philosophy.')

If we end up convinced that there is some reasonable justification for the scandalous claim made by a man called Jesus to speak in the name of God, at that point the only possible way to proceed is to leave God free to speak himself – in the scriptures and in the gospels – without attempting to supplant him with speculative 'natural reasoning'.

Karl Barth: 'Revelation passes judgment on reason. Those who believe in philosophies or humanistic "religions" are always talking. Those who believe in Jesus as the "word of God" are content to listen.'

But (since all one's cards ought to be laid on the table from the start) there are additional reasons for undertaking this research into 'the Jesus of history', although some people will of course consider it anachronistic or worse. For until a few years ago the views of Bultmann and his followers held sway, and 'anyone rash enough to remember that the earthly life of Christ was of some importance to the Christian faith looked for all the world like a latter-day liberal'. Bultmann in fact maintained that it is impossible to deduce anything at all about the Jesus of history.

Some belated discoveries pleasing to 'the powers that be'

We have to confess to being somewhat puzzled (though always ready to revise our ideas should this be proved necessary) to find some Christians now dredging up century-old arguments about the non-historicity of the gospels – arguments that were dear to the Enlightenment, positivism and bourgeois liberalism.

Starting from a right and proper acknowledgment that the gospels are not 'history' in the modern sense (as we shall see in a later chapter) they tend to slide into acceptance of the theory that the gospels are by now historically indefensible. They see no future in trying to establish a valid relation between the Jesus of history and the Jesus of faith.

Such an attitude seems to me not only outdated but also a trifle pathetic, particularly at a time when so many of the theories about the origins of Christianity advanced by bourgeois laicism have fallen into disrepute; and, what is more, at a time when some Marxist scholars are openly declaring that the problem of Jesus needs to be tackled all over again from the beginning.

Catholic scholars now seem to be opening up paths already well trodden at the turn of the century by many allegedly liberal spirits – paths very often abandoned by those old-time wayfarers because they were found to lead nowhere. And yet, to one's surprise, those who now venture along those same paths are considered in some quarters to be 'the avant-garde'.[3]

More than a century after Renan they are again resorting to the demythologising practised by him and many others, to the great satisfaction of the secular authorities concerned as always to safeguard their own cult of power, 'political atheism'. Some genuinely committed theologians (who in many ways deserve all one's respect) seem to forget how Renan, having turned Jesus into a harmless wandering minstrel, was raised to the status of a national hero, the glory of his country. Showered with honours and decorations by the régime, made one of the 'immortals' of the Académie Française, Renan was the favoured protégé of the urban bourgeoisie, the provincial lawyers and the more sophisticated landowners.

Similar good fortune awaited contemporaries of his who were no less committed to trying to emasculate Christianity by excising all its supernatural elements and turning it into a vague religious nostalgia admirably suited to sacralisation of the values dear to the Establishment. Something very similar happened in Germany, where academics like Harnack attracted the admiration and patronage of the Kaisers.

Almost as if to stress the politico-social importance of his attempt to undermine the historical foundations of Christianity, at the end of his work Renan wrote:

'By presiding over what happened at Calvary, the state inflicted the most grievous wound on itself. A legend full of subversive ideas won the day and spread over the whole world. In this legend, the rightful authorities are the villains of the piece, the accused has right on his side, the judges and the forces of law and order conspire against the truth. Seditious to the highest degree ... the story of the passion shows the Roman eagles sanctioning the cruellest of all deaths, soldiers putting it into effect, and a governor issuing the order for it. What a wound inflicted on all constitutional power!'

Whether this merely surprised Renan or whether it deeply disturbed him one cannot tell. But the powers that be did not need to worry any longer; for Renan and his like had declared this seditious hotch-potch to be nothing but 'legend' and had done their best to prove that it was definitely not history, as had been thought for far too long. The 'powers', which had sent Jesus to his death, could now appropriate his cross and wield it like a cudgel, making it the symbol of a 'religion' that is on the side of property and the owners thereof. Not the symbol of a man whom one modern sociologist has classified as 'a criminal type' (in that he attacked the accepted values of the established order), a dangerous 'deviant' whose name was considered a threat to civilised society for the first three centuries. 'Enemies of the human race' is how Tacitus described the early Christians. 'Atheists', because they denied the gods of the state and the state's wars. St Justin, one of the Fathers of the Church, retorted to the emperor Antonius Pius that, in that particular sense, the accusation of atheism levelled against those who believed in Jesus was fully justified.

Abandonment of the Jesus of history: a temptation for reactionaries

There are grounds for believing that all these attempts to minimise the historical basis of Christianity are in fact a response to reactionary habits of thought; that irrespective of the scholars' intentions they serve as a buttress for a society whose religious ideal is the philosophers' God of common-sense.

The humble but stubborn adherence of a believer to his absurd faith, his *stultitia crucis* which has always been folly in the eyes of the powerful and wise of this world, has in it a disruptive force that has long been a source of disquiet for lawful authority. Here is a man who declares all human power to derive from the power of the devil; how can one possibly concede that this man is *also* God?

Luke's gospel, chapter 4: *'The devil showed him all the kingdoms of the world in a single moment, and said to him: "I will give you all this power and all their glory, for it has been ceded to me and I give it to whomever I will; so if you will bow down before me, it shall all be yours." But Jesus said in answer: "It is written: You shall worship the Lord your God, and him only shall you serve".'*

The fears of those who wield power can be set at rest only by turning a faith that spurns purely human values and power-structures into a cultural tradition that conforms with the values and structures of the dominant society's traditions.

Only if the God of Jesus is turned into a legend, only if he loses historical validity – and with it the power his message has to upset ordinary values – is there any hope of going back to the cosily reassuring God of the philosophers. The one who is on the side of the powers that be; not the untameable one who was sent to his death by those powers.

If the God of Abraham who (to the believer) revealed himself in Jesus no longer stands up to examination (to the modern historian), well then there is hope of going back to the God of deism.

If the cross is shown to be merely the symbol of some insubstantial and world-weary 'religious nostalgia'; if it is merely the sign of a legend of some sort that modern historians have no use for, and not a positive reminder of the instrument of execution to which the man Jesus was nailed on the orders of Pontius Pilate, Tiberius' representative in Judaea; if the cross is just another of the countless symbols in religious folklore – then there will be no objection to its display in full view of those in power. Always provided that one goes on promising them that it will bring them victory. ...

It is for these reasons too (over and above the more 'scientific' ones – if that ambiguous adjective has any real meaning) that we reject current attempts to make the Jesus of history socially 'presentable'. When believers take to doing that to him, they in effect deny him.

The historical worth of the New Testament certainly has to be precisely assessed; textual criticism performs a function that is of inestimable value to the faith, and nothing can replace it. Much has to be 're-read', as we shall see when we come to examine fresh ways of understanding the content of the Christian 'belief hypothesis'. So we regret that, in the past especially, many believers have failed to acknowledge their debt of gratitude to so-called sceptics who have contributed, often decisively, to better understanding of the problems surrounding the origins of Christianity.

Nonetheless, we want to go on to consider those origins without adopting the *a priori* stance chosen by so many: 'It is impossible for this to have happened.'

Notes

1 The document in which Vatican I stated that 'God, the beginning and end of all things, can be known with certainty from created reality' went on to say that only through a divine revelation can man succeed in reaching authentic certainty about the divine reality. So the Catholic position on the one hand stresses the fundamental unity between faith and reason, and on the other hand lays equal stress on the insufficiency *in actual fact* of human reason. Thus the revelation of Jesus is not turned into something that merely complements reason and the wisdom of this world (which is 'folly to God', according to Paul in his first letter to the Corinthians).

2 We shall return more than once to this key question of the contrast between the God of Judaism and Christianity and the God of every other monotheistic religion, whether 'religious' or 'philosophical'. We in fact believe that a series of consequences disastrous for Christianity can be traced back to the ambiguous identification of the God of Abraham and Jesus with the God of the philosophers and scientists.

3 In point of fact many Christian theologians, even some of the most up-to-date of them, are still influenced by a training that included a great deal of Greek philosophy. For the Greeks (and for the world of antiquity in general) this world was subject to a Law, a Destiny, a Fate that nobody can flee from – not even Zeus/Jove, for he too was subject to the *Logos*, the mind of the cosmos against which all are powerless. Greek and Roman mythology often depicted the gods shedding tears over the fate of men but unable to intervene. Only Hebrew thought was able to detach itself from that mentality.

God, who created the world and its laws, is in no way subject to those laws himself; he is completely free to suspend, break or reverse them. God's will is so utterly free that it is at liberty even to go back on itself: an ancient Hebrew prayer runs 'Blessed are you, O God, who will what is forbidden'. So it is understandable that theologians who are more familiar with Aristotle than with the Bible are sometimes ill at ease when faced by this Gospel (with all its miracles one after the other leading up to the final miracle of the Resurrection) which is so alien to the Greek mind.

The Hellenic 'law of nature' led eventually to that idol fashioned by nineteenth-century positivism – 'scientific thought'. (The extent to which it can at times be indeed 'scientific' we shall see later.) Among the worshippers of this idol can be counted those who, while professing to believe in the God of the Bible, try to make the gospels 'presentable' by pruning them of anything unacceptable to 'science' as understood by the nineteenth-century cult.

3.

. . . at first foretold . . .

Starting with Moses and then going through all the prophets, he explained to them the passages throughout the scriptures that referred to himself.
LUKE 24, 27

Messianic prophecies as data

Was Jesus in fact foretold? Is it possible, today, to 'check his credentials' by referring back to the Old Testament prophecies?

In the scriptures that are common to both Jews and Christians there are more than 300 'messianic texts'. They foretell the coming of a mysterious figure who will stem from Israel but whose dominion will extend over all peoples and nations. Much is said about what he will do in the world and about the meaning of his appearance in it. Even the date of his coming is, we are told, predicted.

The messianic hope is fundamental to Judaism. The 12th Article of Israel's confession of faith, defined in the Middle Ages by Moses Maimonides, affirms: 'God will send the Messiah,[1] foretold by the Prophets.'

Those among the Jews who acknowledged Jesus as the Messiah believed in him because they were convinced that in him the ancient prophecies were fulfilled. When the earliest Christian preachers addressed the Jewish crowds, they continually had recourse to the argument from prophecy. Matthew's gospel, the one which seems to reflect what was preached to the Jews, continually compares Jesus's actions and sayings with the scriptural predictions. According to Luke, Jesus himself *'explained the passages throughout the scriptures that referred to himself*' in order to convince the Emmaus disciples that he really was the Christ.

Does all this still hold good today?

A two-edged weapon

The argument from prophecy is nowadays widely discredited because too many Christian apologists have misused it. Attempts have been made, some of them merely laughable but others grossly dishonest, to force or twist a passage's meaning so as to prove that in Jesus 'all was fulfilled'. Not to mention the deplorable racist interpretations that condemned Israel unheard.

Modern biblical study has proved that a messianic interpretation of many passages in the Bible does not stand up to examination: sometimes because it can be proved that the writer was alluding to somebody totally different; sometimes because the translations have been shown to be faulty; sometimes because the dating of the books – on which many shaky constructions were based – has turned out to be mistaken. Conflicting translations and textual obscurities had been left out of account, and some quite fantastic allegories and far-fetched analogies had been pressed into service.

Here too the hiddenness of God has too often been forgotten. 'What do the prophets say about Jesus? That he will, manifestly, be God? No. They say that he will be a truly hidden God; that he will go unrecognised; that he will not be thought to be the one who was to come; that he will be a stumbling-block for many. So let people not accuse us of lack of clarity, for we lay no claim to clarity' (Pascal).

The argument from prophecy is a precision instrument that is two-edged – as Christian apologetics has learned to its cost. Especially when it has gone to the length of maintaining, to take just one example, that Jesus was born in a stable between an ox and an ass because the prophet Isaiah (who was obviously speaking of something quite different) had written: *'The ox knows its master and the ass knows its owner's manger.'*

So there has been an understandable reaction against using this means of testing the validity of what is believed, even though according to the gospels Jesus himself more than once suggested it. And there is no denying that in their writings the evangelists and apostles (St Paul in his letters particularly) applied to the prophecies an exegetical method that at times now looks scientifically unsound.

A point in history

However, it seems to us that the problem is less one of seeking the 'telling' verse, or the point of detail that indeed 'came to pass', than of trying to locate Jesus within history.

Before one can get at all close to him one has to pinpoint where he stands in relation to the whole of human existence. His significance cannot be properly understood if one looks only at his own short earthly life – a life that nonetheless found its way into the records of a remote provincial city of the Roman empire.

But if we try to regard him in relation to what preceded him and what followed him – in the light of what Christian theology calls the 'history of salvation' – we may discover how right Hegel was to say that 'all history pivots around Christ'.

The 'mystery of Jesus' would then seem to have its allotted place within a series of 'mysteries' in history that still await plausible explanations. Jesus, and the faith that has its origins in him, seem then to constitute not simply a few minor coincidences but the realisation of the entire Jewish hope, the emergence of that new order of things which had for so long been predicted.

In the pages that follow we shall take a few tentative steps along those lines, trying to extract from the scriptural material some representative 'samples' the content of which is, as far as possible, beyond question.

At all costs we shall avoid the mistake made by those who appeal to arguments from faith in order to kindle faith.

Obviously no single venture of this kind can ever succeed in being convincing for everybody, not only because of the shortcomings and weaknesses of any undertaking of this type but also because certain rules apply when one is dealing with the infinite.

In order that faith may remain what it is, and not get turned into some sort of experimental science, there are both light enough and darkness enough in all the enigmatic signs given by a God who invites discovery of himself and yet never forces anybody to surrender to the evidence.

Pascal: 'The method adopted by God, who is gentle in all that he does, is to bring faith to the intellect by way of reason and to the heart by way of grace.'

There is nothing to stop people writing books the reverse of this one to demonstrate that 'belief is impossible'; plenty have done so and plenty do so still. It should never be forgotten that Christianity can be either accepted or rejected.

There would seem to be a need to begin by tackling two preliminary questions. First the so-called *disbelief of the Jews*, and then the *genuineness of the texts.*

The Jews did believe

It is at least a partial falsification on the part of factious historians and theologians to assert that Israel did not recognise and acknowledge, in Jesus, the Messiah it had been preaching and awaiting for centuries.

All the Nazarene's earliest disciples were Jews. The message was carried the length and breadth of the Roman empire thanks to the belief of a Jewish community. The most active propagator of the Christian Gospel was Saul, the apostle who was *'circumcised on the eighth day, of the race of Israel, the tribe of Benjamin, a Hebrew of Hebrew parentage'* as he himself declared. All the earliest documents of the new faith testify to thousands of conversions among the people of Israel. The Church of Rome, the Church of the Pope, originated with the thousands of Jews brought there by Pompey as slaves and subsequently freed.

Towards the year 250 a Christian writer, Origen, estimated the number of Jewish Christians at around 150,000; and he was probably speaking of recent conversions only. The figure is remarkable, for it represents a very high percentage of the total. Even a century later, when paganism had succumbed, Christians were still a minority in the empire, and were to be found only among the urban populations. The Church was so predominantly Jewish in the early centuries that the most emotive question it had to settle was which of the traditional Jewish customs it should retain. This we shall see later, especially in regard to circumcision.

The fact is that Judeo-Christianity is virtually a closed book to all but a few specialists. Only recently has it been studied at all seriously. This neglect has been due to anti-Semitism on the part of western Christians who found it convenient to conceal the truth about the origins of the Church. What other explanation is there for the sort of theology that misguidedly spoke of an Israel 'repudiated by God'? There have always been plenty of people who find it embarrassing to have to admit that Jesus was Jewish. In our own time, Nazism tried to detach Jesus from his own people by reviving the old tale that invented a Roman centurion as his father, thus making him an 'Aryan' after all. ...

In reality, as Julien Green has written, 'it is impossible to strike a Jew without striking the one who is not only perfect man but also the flower of Israel'.

That Jewish 'disbelief' is largely mythical is confirmed by one of the most notable representatives of present-day religious thought, Jules Isaac, an impressive defender of the innocence of his own people as well as an apostle of dialogue between Judaism and Christianity. In his view the relationship between the two faiths is that of mother and daughter. He has said:

'Christian writers forget that by Jesus's day the Jewish dispersion (the Diaspora) had been a fait accompli for several centuries. The greater part of the Jewish people no longer lived in Palestine. So it cannot be said that the majority of the Jewish people rejected Jesus. Indeed it is highly probable that the majority of the Jewish people knew nothing about him. But, wherever Jesus did go – with rare exceptions – the Jewish people gave him an enthusiastic hearing, as the gospels show. Did this people in fact turn against him at one point in time? It is said that they did, but it cannot be proved that they did. ... The people of Israel is the only people among whom Jesus found, side by side with bitter enemies, fervent disciples and crowds who adored him.'

The hateful anti-Semitic myth of 'an unbelieving people repudiated by God' and consequently 'accursed' is therefore both historically and theologically baseless. As Isaac has remarked: 'to call oneself at one and the same time both anti-Semitic and Christian is to mix insult in with veneration'. And Karl Barth, perhaps the greatest Christian theologian of this century, has pointedly observed that Nazism's anti-Jewish stance was ample evidence that Nazism was fundamentally anti-Christian. The two faiths are intimately linked to a single destiny: Christ cut off from Israel is not Christian.

In the first place, therefore, the contemptuous teaching about the Jews propagated by Christians down the centuries is quite simply absurd. Indeed, as Daniélou has commented, Christian belief in the ideas of 'salvation history', 'divine election' and 'divine revelation' ought to make Christians especially appreciative of the reason why the Jewish people is a quite exceptional people.

In the second place, the argument often used by those who

would like to disregard the messianic prophecies altogether is equally untenable; this is the argument that runs: How could Jesus have been 'the one who was to come', given that his own people who preserved and studied those prophecies did not acknowledge him as such?

Many Jews who knew him and listened to his message did believe in him as the fulfilment of the ancient prophecies. So much so that, according to the gospels, he was often obliged to retreat into hiding in order to escape from the enthusiasm of the crowds.

After his final disappearance, Paul and the other apostles turned their attention first of all to their Jewish compatriots who had settled abroad. Scripture in hand, they 'proved' Jesus on the basis of those very prophecies. And the results were by no means meagre: many crossed the threshold from Judaism into Christianity. For them it was no 'new' religion but a natural development of the old faith.

If the preachers often came up against a solid wall of obduracy, it seems that this was due less to lack of agreement concerning the validity of argument from prophecy than to *a priori* refusal on the part of the Jewish communities' leaders to engage in any sort of dialogue.

One present-day Jewish historian, Sam Waagenar, has indicated what may well have been said to anyone trying to prove that Jesus was the Christ: "We know that the proclamation of the messianic era is to be made in Jerusalem. No proclamation of the coming of the Messiah has reached us from Jerusalem. Therefore the man you are talking about is an impostor. It is both useless and blasphemous to consult the prophets about him."

Faced with that sort of reasoning, the new arrivals naturally had to abandon all hope of 'examining the scriptures together'. Unable to break down the resistance, the Christians eventually turned their attention to the 'pagans'. And so began the digging of that deep dividing trench which was to have tragic consequences for Christianity itself for nearly two thousand years.

Sometimes a very curious brand of logic is detectable in criticism that claims to be 'reasoned'. We shall find plenty of examples of this later on. For the time being let us take a look at two arguments 'from reason' often adopted by reputable New Testament scholars – almost always German. Oddly enough, both arguments are often to be found in works by one and the same author in spite of the fact that they are mutually exclusive.

On the one hand it is asserted (with little or no historical justification, as we have seen) that 'The prophecies alleged to have been fulfilled in Jesus must have been given a twist; for the authors of them, the Jews, did not recognise and acknowledge him; this is definitive proof of the weakness of the arguments from prophecy adduced by Christians.'

On the other hand it is said that 'It is entirely logical that Jesus, historically nothing but an obscure Galilean preacher, should have been mistaken for God. Though only a man he was endowed with divinity by the faith of pious Jews who believed they could see in him the fulfilment of their prophecies and the realisation of their hopes.'

In the first theory, the over-credulous ones are Christians of pagan origin who are supposed to have interpreted the Old Testament prophecies in ways all their own.

In the second theory (which underlies a great deal of New Testament study) the over-credulous ones are Jews who are supposed to have given too much credence to the messianic prophecies.

Who, then, is to be held responsible for the 'colossal misunderstanding' that has grown up around Jesus? Some Christians who failed to appreciate the ironies of subtle Jewish thought? Or a few Jews who, using make-believe 'tests', are supposed to have persuaded a number of simpletons into believing in their Messiah?

Clearly the two theories cancel one another out. And yet together they are the props and stays of a number of weighty conclusions about the origins of Christianity.

One book that is above suspicion

One thing nobody has ever been able to say is that the messianic prophecies themselves (whatever their value) were adulterated by those who preached Christ. No critic has ever been able to plunge his scalpel into the Old Testament declaring: "This passage has been interpolated by Christians."

That suspicion certainly has been entertained about every other text that includes even the remotest reference to Jesus. But it has always been out of the question in regard to the Old Testament – for one excellent reason.

Wherever and whenever the Christians' Messiah has been the subject of dispute, there have always been Jews near at hand intent on preserving the integrity of their own holy writ.

For Christians, it is now simply the Old Testament, scripture that has been completed and overtaken by the New. But it is nonetheless scripture, in which anyone wanting to do so can find the prophecies relating to the Messiah.

You may be convinced by them or you may not. But you are bound to concede that the survival of the Jewish people, and their tenacious safeguarding of their Book, have enabled you to delve into texts that have definitely not been tampered with.

Pascal saw as providential the handing-down to us of a Scripture that has been kept thoroughly 'genuine' thanks to the unconquerable resistance of one nation: "If the entire Jewish people had been converted by Jesus Christ, we would have no documents that are not suspect. And if the Jewish people had been wiped out, we would have no documents at all."

Moreover in 1947, in a cave at Qumran near the Dead Sea, came the discovery of a complete text of one of the major prophets, Isaiah. That scroll dates from at least one century before Christ; yet, apart from a few details of punctuation, the text is identical with that of the Bibles on sale in our twentieth-century bookshops.

It is unique for one faith to be in a position to look for its credentials among the texts that another faith has preserved intact. Yet it is undeniable fact. And it brings us back to the unique relationship between the two faiths.

From the beginning of history, Jesus has been either foretold or adored

What distinguishes Christianity from any other faith is that *it is a religion worshipping a Messiah and founded on another religion predicting that same Messiah.*

As Pascal remarks, both the Old Testament and the New set all their sights on Jesus: 'The Old awaits him, the New extols him; for both he is at the heart of all things.' So, 'this religion which consists in believing that mankind fell from a state of glory and communion with God to a state of separation from God, but that after this present life we shall be restored to our original condition by a Messiah whose coming is decreed, – well, this religion has always existed on earth. All else has had its day, and this alone has gone on existing.'

From the beginning of written history until the present day, *Jesus has always been either foretold or adored.*

Buddha, Confucius, Lao-Tse, Mohammed – all the other founders of religions are isolated figures, historically speaking. No religious tradition preceding them foretells their arrival; they just appear, unannounced.

By contrast, Jesus is the focal point of one surge of expectation that preceded him (lasting perhaps as long as eighteen or twenty centuries but certainly not less than twelve) and another surge of adoration that followed him. For the last twenty centuries the Church has been carrying forward the work pioneered by the synagogue.

A development such as this one, spanning perhaps as

many as forty centuries, defies all the laws that govern historical phenomena. What is more, this Messiah was predicted not by one single isolated prophet but by a whole series of men who for centuries proclaimed the same prophecy and little by little developed it more fully.

Jesus's position is absolutely unique, we must repeat. According to many scholars, this uniqueness is in itself enough to win for Christianity a place completely apart from the other world religions.

The 'sons of Abraham' number 1,300 million

Jews, Christians and Muslims all call themselves 'sons of Abraham'. If the statistics are reliable they together amount to a religious grouping encompassing about thirteen hundred million human beings.

Jews believe that their race is descended from Abraham through his son Isaac.

Christians are told by Paul: "Abraham is the father of us all."

For a long time Muslims called themselves 'Ishmaelites', that is to say descendants of Ishmael, son of Abraham and Hagar.

God is said by the Bible to have made a promise to a man called Abraham. The promise was recorded in writing by Hebrew authors many centuries before Jesus or Mohammed. What is more they recorded it at a time when Israel was only a small, despised, semi-nomad people, lost in a Middle East in which powerful and sophisticated empires abounded.

Let us look at the first of the scriptural books, Genesis, chapter 12: *'Now the Lord God said to Abraham: "Go from your country and your kindred and your father's house to the land that I will show you. And I will make of you a great nation, and I will bless you and make your name glorious, so that you will be a blessing. ... In you all the families of the earth will be blessed".'*

Still in Genesis, chapter 15: *'Then (the Lord) brought him outside and said to him: "Look towards heaven and count the stars, if you can." And he added: "So shall your descendants be." And he (Abraham) believed; and for this God accounted him righteous.'*

Further on, in chapter 18, the author makes God say: *"Abraham shall become a great and powerful nation, and all the nations of the earth shall be blessed in him."*

These, then, are promises of endless fecundity. It was no accident that the name Abraham means, literally, 'father of a multitude (of nations)'.

Now, many centuries after these predictions were written down, the followers of the faiths which claim Abraham as their father can be counted in thousands of millions; in 1976 these 'descendants' of the earliest of Israelite patriarchs made up about 43% of the world population. And the Bible, the book which tells of Israel's trust in the unimaginable promise, had by then been translated into 1,120 languages and dialects. It is far and away *the* best-seller of all time.

Unshakeable belief in a permanent role of world importance

Whether Abraham ever existed or not is of no importance whatever. What does matter (and it is undeniable fact) is the astonishing megalomania that caused an entire people, few in number and lacking power, to go on predicting for itself a future role of world importance. Moreover, at least ten centuries before Christianity and sixteen centuries before Islam, it set down this conviction in writing – an all-absorbing conviction which might appear to spring from a fevered imagination but which events were to confirm in a totally unexpected fashion.

Throughout her history as recorded by her in the Bible, Israel never entertained any doubts about the mysterious role entrusted to her by God. (Incidentally, according to one interpretation believed to be etymologically sound, the name Israel means 'defender of God'.) This people, negligible in size but bursting with vigour, has certainly lived up to the role God is said to have entrusted to it at the dawn of history: "*You shall be for me a kingdom of priests and a holy nation*" (Exodus 19).

Here we can give only a few examples, from the many in the Bible, of this firm conviction that defies explanation.

In Genesis, chapter 49, Isaac's son Jacob is on his deathbed, about to give his sons his blessing: "*Gather together, that I may declare to you what will happen to you in time to come.*" Jacob says: "*The sceptre shall not be taken from Judah, nor the mace from between his feet, until the coming of Him to whom it belongs, and to Him shall go the obedience of the nations.*"

Is Jesus the one to whom *the obedience of the nations* shall be given? Christians believe that he is; and we have it on good authority that Jewish exegetes have always read the passage in a messianic sense.

Chapter 7 of the second book of Samuel records the promise God is said to have had conveyed to David: "*When your days have run their full course and you are laid to rest with your ancestors, I will preserve your offspring after you and make his sovereignty secure. It is he who will build a house devoted to my name, and I shall see to it that his royal throne will endure for ever. ... Your house and your sovereignty will always stand secure in my sight, your throne will stand firm for ever. ...*"

The textual critics have suggested several different interpretations of this passage. Faith counsels caution in the matter, given that God is a hidden God. We refrain in any case from making the point that according to the gospel-writers Jesus was a descendant of David; for that at once invites one perfectly logical objection, i.e. that the gospel-writers could easily have tailored his genealogy to fit the prophecy. We prefer to remain on firm ground – in this case remarking only that here again a people affirms its belief that it will endure for ever and expresses its inexplicable conviction that it is to play a permanent and decisive role in the history of mankind.

Let us now look at one of the last Old Testament books to be written, the book of Daniel who (according to its chapter 7) *'in the first year of Belshazzar, King of Babylon, had a dream and visions that passed through his head as he lay in bed'.* This was the prophecy of the four beasts, about which we shall have more to say later. In it we read: *'I was gazing into the visions of the night when I saw, coming on the clouds of heaven, one like a son of man. He came to the Ancient of days* (God, the Eternal one) *and was led into his presence. To him were given dominion, honour and sovereignty, and men of all peoples, nations and languages served him. His dominion is an eternal dominion that will never pass away, and his sovereignty is such as will never be destroyed.'*

Ever since the apostles' time the Church has perceived here, too, a proclamation of her Messiah. Especially noteworthy is the nature of the promised universal sovereignty: *'such as will never be destroyed'.* Just the kind of sovereignty that Jesus chose for himself, a sovereignty not over earthly kingdoms but over men's hearts.

In the book of the prophet Isaiah there appears an enigmatic figure called 'the servant of the Lord'. The destiny predicted for him is one in which glory and humiliation are mingled in a way that seems quite incomprehensible. In chapter 49 the author makes God say that for this 'servant' there is more to come than sovereignty over Israel: *"To be my servant it is not enough for you to restore the tribes of Jacob and bring back the survivors of Israel! I will make you the light of the nations, so that you may carry my salvation to the ends of the earth."*

This passage is of particular interest: it seems as though Isaiah wanted to give an unwavering answer to the more prudent Jews who envisaged a Messiah who would merely restore the kingdom of Israel. That, after all, was a realistic, common-sense view; for how could a people as wretched as theirs possibly expect to influence the entire world? But the prophet will have none of that: he proclaims that the King who will arise will be *'the light of all the nations'*.

As for Jerusalem, Isaiah prophesies in chapter 60 that it will become *the light and centre of the world.* Here is what is predicted of a city that was then little more than a humble mountain village, laughable as a capital in comparison with the splendid cities of the ancient world: *'Arise, shine out, for your light has come, the glory of the Lord is resplendent above you. Though night still covers the earth and dense cloud the peoples, the Lord in his splendour is over you and his glory is appearing above you. All the nations shall come to your light and the kings to your shining splendour.'* And again the prophecy ends with a promise of glory for Israel: *'The least among you will become a people and the smallest a powerful nation. I am the Lord; in due time I shall act speedily.'*

One last quotation from among the many that speak of the coming of the Messiah, from the book of Micah, chapter 4: *'In the days to come* (i.e. when the One who is awaited arrives) *the mountain of the house of the Lord will be raised to the summit of the mountains and lifted higher than the hills, and the peoples will flow to it. Many nations will run towards it saying: "Come, let us go to the mountain of the Lord, to the house of the God of Jacob. He will teach us his ways and we shall walk along his paths." Because out of Zion shall go forth the law and the word of the Lord from Jerusalem.'*

Yahweh, a God whom the human sciences fail to explain

Here, then, we find a small ethnic group who since the very beginning of their history had pinned their faith on the future; they expected a *'blessing for their race'* and looked forward to an everlasting Kingdom established by One of themselves. So certain were they of all this that some of their commentaries on the Scriptures went so far as to declare that the world was created for Israel and without Israel the world would cease to exist.

We may well be amazed by the certainty they displayed. But what is even more amazing – today more than ever – is the origin of this belief. How in fact can one possibly find an explanation for Yahweh, the God of Israel?

This God – and he is also the one Christians believe to have manifested himself in Jesus – is deeply shrouded in mystery; and he confounds all the laws that scientific thought would have us believe applicable to every religion.

The progress made in the last couple of centuries in the study of comparative religion has served only to deepen the mystery of the origin of Jewish belief.

What was the source of its uncompromising monotheism? All the ancient religions – not only those of the Mediterranean and the East but also those of Africa, America and Australasia – were polytheistic. Why was it that the Jews, from the very start of their history, imagined the heavens to be populated not by a multitude of gods but by one God only? The researchers into comparative religion tell us that such a concept of divinity is *always the outcome of a long evolution in religious thought.* Yet this people would seem to have thought monotheistically from the start, without needing to go through the lengthy processes normally leading up to monotheism. It is as if their sacred scriptures were right in asserting that Israel neither invented nor chose her God but that God chose his people and revealed himself to their patriarchs.

Franz König, an expert in the sociology of religion, has written: 'The more we get to know about the religious history and culture of the Orient of antiquity, and the more we understand how the various religions influenced one another, the more puzzled we become by Israel's monotheistic concept of God which contrasts so strongly with the completely polytheistic concepts of all her neighbours.' In 1960 the historian Y. Kaufmann published an eight-volume work showing that 'Jewish monotheism remains a phenomenon that defies investigation and research. Here we stand on the threshold of one of the deepest mysteries in history.'

But Tacitus had already expressed the stupefaction felt by the ancient world when it encountered that extraordinarily 'different' Judaism: 'Moses raised up a people that endures to this day, giving them rites and observances that were not only new but contrary to those of all other peoples – *novos ritus contrariosque ceteris mortalibus.*'

Besides being inexplicable quantitatively, Israel's monotheism is inexplicable qualitatively as well. The problem is not simply one of number – the one God as opposed to many gods.

Rabbi Isidore Epstein, Principal of the Jews' College in London, has observed: 'as Creator of heaven and earth and all therein, the God of Abraham is independent of nature and every geographical limitation'.

The Jewish concept of a universal deity was in itself unique; in the other old religious systems each god was thought of as a 'local' god, a god of the people or of the city, *never the God of the universe.*

Moreover, the God of Israel was not only *the one God, the universal God.* He was an ethical God, concerned above all with holiness and justice.

This lies at the heart of the enigma presented by Judaism. The command 'Be holy' addressed to mankind is based on the conviction that God himself is holy.

'The Lord spoke to Moses saying: "Speak to the whole assembly of Israel, and say to them: Be holy, for I, the Lord your God, am holy"' (Leviticus 19). *"Cease to do evil, learn to do good. Seek justice, and help the oppressed"* (Isaiah 1).

If men are required to be just in their dealings with one

another, it is because God himself is justice: *'The holy God shows himself holy by his justice'* (Isaiah 5).

This holy and just God, in whom men are to see the model for their own behaviour, is the very opposite of the deities conceived by the other religions of antiquity. Polytheism's gods had all the human strengths and weaknesses: caprice alone decided whether they granted men favours or turned against them in outbursts of rage.

So Israel's God was totally 'different', and the refinements of modern research are powerless to explain how the difference came about.

This strangely original concept of *the one and only, universal, holy, just God* was not confined to an aristocratic or intellectual élite; it was shared by a whole people.

Furthermore, it infinitely surpassed the concepts of Israel's contemporaries even though in every other respect Israel was obviously outclassed by her neighbours. Her religious insight was unrivalled, but her inferiority in everything else – the arts, philosophy, law, technology – was clear for all to see.

One present-day archaeologist has said that we would have a 'ludicrous' image of the Israel of antiquity if we had only excavations to provide us with knowledge about her – as is the case with so many other ancient civilisations. Artistically and architecturally she was undoubtedly poor; her greatness lay in her Bible, that 'history of a faith'.

The human sciences have yet to explain this gross inconsistency; it is one more problem posed by a people that seems to have been exempt from the law of history which asserts that development of a community's religious tradition goes hand-in-hand with the people's overall cultural development.

Israel's lived experience buttressed Israel's faith: the belief that God himself intervenes in history so as to reveal aspects of himself that are beyond the reach of human wisdom; the belief that Israel did not choose its God but that God himself chose Israel and granted Israel the privilege of a unique revelation.

But there is more to be said about this God who becomes less and less explicable as research becomes more and more 'advanced'.

God, man and the natural world

The very first words of scripture (*'In the beginning, Yahweh created heaven and earth'*, Genesis 1, 1) contain teaching about Israel's God. And it is teaching that flatly rejected the assumptions underlying every other religion of antiquity. A clear-cut distinction is at once made between God and nature; and along with this goes an equally clear distinction between man and nature too.

In the other ancient religious traditions, man lived in a sort of spell-ridden forest in which caverns and woodlands were alive with spirits. Rocks and rivers swarmed with demons, some more ill-disposed to men than others. The whole of the visible and tangible world was in the grip of some magic power. Even to the Babylonians, masters of human knowledge in the East of the time, the moon and the stars were divine beings.

Yet to Israel, that uncultured bunch of uncouth shepherd tribes, the sun and the moon and everything in the world were no more than things – things created by the one and only, all-encompassing, eternal God. Only for Israel was nature emptied of all magic and the world set free from ceaseless agitation by demons and spirits.

'The prohibition of nature-worship implicit in the first commandment (*"You shall have no other God but me"*) and the corresponding prohibition of idol-making give Israel's monotheism its distinctive character, setting the God of Israel totally apart from any other concept of God, whether polytheistic or monotheistic' (Epstein).

It is this concept that enables man, freed from primitive terrors, to shape his own destiny in harmony with the will of God. Only in Hebrew thought did man collaborate with God in the work of creation – in the activity of the boundless spirit who daily and unceasingly renews the work of creation.

Hebrew mystics have gone as far as saying that 'God needs man just as man needs God' – an assertion that is blasphemous in the eyes of Muslims to this day.

The uniqueness of this Hebrew view of the world amid the otherwise sacral and magical traditions of antiquity has still not been satisfactorily explained by any human science. That 'demythologisation' effected by the earliest religious thinkers in Israel, and accepted by the entire people, is yet another of history's enigmas. One of the many presented by that mysterious people from whom Christianity sprang.

History as a progression

A closer look at Hebrew religious thought leads to further discoveries.

By introducing the ideas of a messianic future, of a new heaven and a new earth, of a people making its way towards new goals, Judaism made yet another radical departure. For the cultures of antiquity, history constantly repeated itself in an endless succession of closed circles within which man was held prisoner, condemned to tread the same path for ever with no possibility of escape. The idea of progression was unknown to the East, to Greece and to Rome; modern culture owes it to the old Israel.

For the Jews history was a sign pointing towards growth and development. As one Israeli scholar has written: 'Judaism has never looked back to days gone by; the golden age is not past but still to come. Perfection lies at history's end' (Dante Lattes). This is the exact opposite of Graeco-Roman thought, which time and again indulged in nostalgia for 'the good old days'.

So here again is a concept found only among a few semi-nomad tribes in a remote corner of the Middle East – an idea that the advanced cultures of classical antiquity failed to conceive.

A changeless God

So from a scientific standpoint both the origin and the content of Jewish belief are insoluble enigmas.

But its development, too, defies scientific explanation.

According to modern anthropological science, religions evolve and develop in obedience to certain 'laws'; but one after another those 'laws' are set at nought by the faith of the people of Israel. Just as they do not explain Judaism's original unprecedented monotheism, so they fail to account for the survival of this one and only God when Israel ceased to be a bunch of nomadic shepherd tribes and became instead a settled agricultural, stock-rearing people.

The anthropologists tell us that whenever economic changes of that kind occur, the 'local' gods and tribal gods are abandoned in favour of gods of the crops and fertility cults.

Certainly there is evidence in the Old Testament that the people were more than once tempted in that direction. But thanks to the exhortations of their prophets they always resisted the temptation and remained loyal to Yahweh.

The same resistance to natural change occurred when they set up a kingdom. Unlike every other people they did not then devise one of those state religions with gods that are personifications of kingly power, gods whose words and actions are those of political authority and whose function is to endow that authority with additional power by inducing respect for what is sacred. One example of that type of development was the Babylonian god Marduk, the god who 'governed'.

The exact opposite occurred with Israel: the kingdom was seen as Yahweh's creation. He was not the servant but the master of the state. And faith in him survived even the dismantling of the whole state apparatus: even in exile the people remained true to him.

In the midst of nations that put their faith in 'chariots and horses' Israel lived in naked hope and faith in the 'living God', the 'God of Abraham, Isaac and Jacob'.

A survival that fulfils the promise

As we well know, that fidelity to the God of Abraham and Moses has continued to the present day, in spite of everything and everybody.

The Jews are the only people to have kept their identity intact throughout the break-up of the ancient world.

Where now are the Assyrians and Babylonians, the Etruscans and Phoenicians, the Parthians, Macedonians and Carthaginians, even the Greeks and the Romans? What is there left of those peoples who seemed, in their heyday, to have far more solid ethnic and cultural bases than the Jews?

In the Tigris and Euphrates basin alone (where Abraham originated) many nations arose, flourished and then disappeared from history within a span of a few thousand years. Not only Assyrians and Babylonians but Sumerians and Akkadians, Amorites and Hittites, Medes and Persians. ... Wars fought and lost, invasions, persecutions spelt for them all the decline and fall of society, culture, religion, the race itself.

For all except the people of Israel.

This endurance may well astonish the student of history. But believers can reflect on what Yahweh assured the Jews in Isaiah, chapter 66: "*For just as the new heavens and the new earth which I shall make will endure, so shall your descendants and your name endure.*"

"We," says one of the Qumran scrolls, "we, sons of Abraham and of Moses, are an everlasting people."[2]

Jesus as the key

It is now time to examine the Hebrew scriptures from a later viewpoint.

Let us move on from the predictions of a Messiah to the fulfilment of those predictions in the one whom Christians believe to be the promised Messiah.

In what sense did Jesus fulfil the prophecies so often repeated in the Old Testament?

And what light does the coming of Christianity throw on the enigmas in Jewish history? And what other 'prophecies' reached fulfilment in that coming?

Vatican II's document on Revelation quotes St Augustine as saying: "God wisely arranged that the New Testament be hidden in the Old and the Old be made manifest in the New."

Christians are convinced that the Gospel alone is the key to the obscurities in the Hebrew Bible's messianic prophecies. Only in Jesus is it possible to reconcile the apparently contradictory features in the portraits the Old Testament paints of 'the One who is to come'.

Notes

1 The word Messiah comes from the Hebrew term *Mashàh, the anointed one.* It was applied to those who were consecrated as high priest or king by an anointing of their heads. For the Jews, the king especially was *Mashàh Yahweh,* 'the Lord's anointed one', above all others. As time went on the term became restricted to the ultimate, supreme King, the one predicted by the prophets.

2 Pascal: 'Nations can endure only if their laws are frequently adapted to circumstances and needs. Judaism, however, has always sustained itself in spite of remaining inflexible.' As the Romans found when their policy of assimilation based on tolerance met with no success: unlike the other nations, the Jews refused to effect any compromise with the Graeco-Latin *ecumene* that then 'united' the Mediterranean basin.

4.

. . . and then adored . . .

They welcomed the message very readily, studying the scriptures every day to check whether it was true.

ACTS 17, 11

Italo Zolli, at one time Chief Rabbi of the Jewish community in Rome, became a Catholic in 1945. His knowledge of scripture has never been disputed. Writing after his conversion to Christianity he had this to say: 'The whole of the Old Testament appears to me like an enciphered telegram sent from God to men. It is quite incomprehensible to anyone attempting to read it without the decipherment key. That key is Christ. In the light of Christ, the thrill of expectancy that runs through all the books of the Old Testament takes on real meaning.'

'The shepherds will change; the flock will grow larger'

We have seen that the ancient scriptures continually proclaim that within the divine plan an enduring and exceptional role is assigned to the Jewish people. But in the self-same prophecies the promise is accompanied by a warning.

Ezekiel, chapter 34: *'The word of the Lord came to me: "Son of man, prophesy against the shepherds of Israel, prophesy and say to them. ... Watch out, shepherds of Israel who have been feeding yourselves! Should not shepherds feed the sheep? ... Thus says the Lord God, Behold I am against the shepherds; and I will take my sheep back from them. ... I myself will search for my sheep and take care of them".'*

So spiritual leadership is one day to pass out of the hands of the priests of Judaism.

Here we seem to have a prediction of that direct intervention of God in history, that entry into the human sphere by the totally 'Other', which is believed and proclaimed by Christians.

Moreover, the new 'flock' will no longer be exclusively Jewish; 'sheep' from all nations will enter it. Ezekiel goes on:

'*"As a shepherd seeks out his flock when some of his sheep have become scattered, so will I seek out my sheep and bring them safely from all the places where they have been scattered on a day of clouds and darkness. I will bring them out from the peoples, and gather them from the countries; and I will bring them back to their land and pasture them on the mountains of Israel, by the rivers and in all the grassy places. ... I myself will feed my sheep, and I myself will shear them, says the Lord God. I will go in search of the lost and I will bring back the strays; I will bandage the wounded and strengthen the weak".'*

Does this predict the 'Good Shepherd', the Jesus in whom Christians believe?

One point needs to be made here. For Christians, Jesus does fulfil this prophecy, and he does so in a way that goes far beyond the Israelite messianic hope. None of the many Jewish theories about the Messiah ever envisaged that God himself would become a man. But Jesus, for those who believe in him, does fulfil Ezekiel's prophecy of a direct intervention by Yahweh himself who becomes the shepherd of his flock.

Furthermore the religion that originates in Jesus does, beyond all doubt, bear out the prophet's warning that the religion of the God of Israel would cease to be the monopoly of the old Israelite priesthood.

Isaiah, chapter 66, also predicts that Yahweh *'will come to gather all the nations and tongues'.* "*And among them too,*" says the Lord, "*I will select for myself priests and levites.*"

So the end of the Jewish monopoly was to lead to the spread of worship and service of the Lord the world over.

Leaving aside all considerations that can be classed as 'of faith', there is no denying that on the purely objective level of historical fact the development predicted a few thousand years ago by the prophets of Israel has taken place. Israel has indeed transmitted religious pre-eminence to a people that sprang originally from her and that claims to have been assembled by God himself when he entered history to become that people's 'shepherd'. That new people of God has grown beyond all expectation and now reaches to the ends of the earth.

There will be a new covenant

The Old Testament also predicts something new in the relationship between God and man.

According to the prophets, the faith is to develop and take on a deeper meaning while remaining true to its origins. There is to be *a new covenant* that will extend as well as renew the old covenant entered into between Yahweh and Israel alone.

Christians believe that their faith fulfils this promise of a new covenant with the God of Moses and Abraham.

Jeremiah, chapter 31: "*Behold, the days are coming, says the Lord, when I will make a new covenant with the house of Israel and the house of Judah. Not like the covenant which I made with their fathers when I took them by the hand to bring them out of the land of Egypt; for they broke that covenant of mine, so I had to show them that I was the Lord, says the Lord. The covenant I shall make with the house of Israel when the time comes will instead be like this, says the Lord: I shall place my law deep within them, I shall write it on their hearts, I shall be their God and they will be my people.*" And Ezekiel, chapter 36: "*I shall give you a new heart and put a new spirit in you; I shall remove from your bodies the heart of stone and give you a heart of flesh. I shall put my spirit in you. ...*"

The passage from Jeremiah is followed by a description of another aspect of this new situation: there will no longer be any need of prophets to proclaim God's will, for men will learn it in a different way. "*And no longer will men teach one another, saying: Learn to know the Lord. For they shall all know me, from the least of them to the greatest, says the Lord, because I shall forgive their iniquities and remember their sin no more.*"

Is Jesus the one who established the *new covenant*, the one who places God's law *deep within them* and writes it *on their hearts?* Is he the one who has superseded the prophets because in him God himself has spoken? That is what history shows to be the case. And faith certainly believes that Jesus is the one through whom the 'new heaven' and the 'new earth' promised by God in Isaiah 66 will come about.

Will the book become 'sealed'?

Throughout the Old Testament, often within a single book and sometimes within a single chapter, Israel's future is foretold in a mixture of promises and threats.

Side by side with the promise of unbelievable growth and extension of the faith, and of its everlasting continuance, we find predictions of loss of religious monopoly and of a new covenant to be entered into with others. And it is also predicted that a sort of blindness will afflict the people and make Israel '*a proverb and a byword among all peoples*', along the lines of the threat in I Kings, chapter 9.

Isaiah 29: '*Indeed the Lord has poured on you a spirit of lethargy; he has closed your eyes and covered your heads. Every vision will therefore be for you like the words of a sealed book: give it to someone who can read and tell him "Read that" and he will reply "I cannot, because it is sealed"; or give it to someone who cannot read and tell him "Read that" and he will reply "I cannot read".'*

According to Isaiah (who elsewhere predicts a glorious future for Israel) God will accomplish *'marvellous prodigies'* against the people: *'the wisdom of its wise men shall perish, and the discernment of its discerning men shall vanish'.*

And in chapter 56, Isaiah's God says that to the despised and the foreigners *"I will give, in my house and within my walls, a monument and a name better than sons and daughters."*

Does this mean that the faith of the Jews will extend over the whole earth, but that Israel will remain everlastingly the *'guardian of the texts and the promises'* without ever deciphering them fully? That is what the prophets of old seem to be saying.

And that is how Christians, from apostolic times, have understood the mysterious destiny of Israel among the nations. In his letter to the Romans Paul says of the Jews: *'I bear them witness that they have a zeal for God, but it is not enlightened'; 'Israel has not understood'; 'God has given them a spirit of stupor, eyes that do not see and ears that do not hear';* at least *'until now'* says Paul.

But there will come a time for the Jews too to recognise Christ: *'My brothers, lest you be wise in your own conceits, I want you to understand this mystery: a hardening has come upon part of Israel, but this will last only until the whole pagan world has entered; and so all Israel will be saved.'*

So Paul foresaw, as early as the year 57–58, that part of Israel would not accept Jesus as the Messiah, and predicted that there would be no change in its attitude until every other people had become Christian.

For Pascal, Judaism's survival was an integral part of a divine plan, a supernatural strategy: 'Israel is clearly a people created expressly to bear witness to the Messiah. It was not enough that the prophecies existed; they had to be disseminated everywhere and preserved for all time.' The fourth chapter of the prophecy of Micah seems to bear Pascal out: *'the word of the Lord will go forth from Jerusalem'*; the one awaited by Israel *'will be judge between many peoples, arbiter among powerful and far-off nations'*; the one *'who is to be ruler in Israel'* will be born at Bethlehem. And then, says Micah, *'the remnant of Jacob* (the Jews, in fact) *shall be in the midst of many peoples like dew from the Lord, like showers upon the grass, expecting nothing from men and hoping for nothing from the sons of men'*.

King of glory and man of sorrows

If the coming of Christianity explains the prophecies in which, for Israel, promise is mingled with threat (and indisputable facts of history do support this view) Jesus himself, through what befell him, resolves the apparent contradictions in the messianic prophecies.

The Old Testament predicts for the Messiah on the one hand the greatest possible glory and on the other hand abject humiliation and suffering. That destiny was Christ's alone.

Here is Isaiah's outstanding prophecy, which both Jews and Christians have always understood as messianic. God begins by saying: *"Behold, my servant shall prosper, he shall be exalted and lifted up and shall rise very high ... he shall astonish many nations, kings will be speechless before him, for they shall see things that have never been told to them, they will understand things they have never heard before."* Yet immediately afterwards the prophecy about that strange Messianic figure 'the servant of Yahweh' changes completely: *"he had neither beauty nor nobility when one saw him, nor any features to attract one. He was despised and rejected by men, a man of sorrows and no stranger to grief; a man from whom one's gaze is averted; he was despised, and we thought nothing of him. But the sufferings he bore were ours, and ours were the sorrows he carried; yet we held him to be stricken, smitten by God and brought low."*

Then come verses which are profoundly moving for the Christian, who sees in them the proclamation of the Passion of Jesus and his role in the destiny of mankind: "*All we like sheep had gone astray, each wandering along his own path; but the Lord let all our sins fall on him. He was cruelly ill-treated but he bore it all with humility, never saying a word: like a lamb that is led to the slaughter, like a sheep confronted with its shearers. Under an oppressive sentence he was taken away. ...*"

But Isaiah's prophecy ends as it began: "*After deep anguish he shall see the light and be filled with knowledge and understanding. My righteous servant will make many righteous, and will take upon himself the burden of their sins. For this I will give him great multitudes as his reward, and the mighty will be to him as booty*" (chapters 52–53).

Another outstanding messianic text, Psalm 22, is placed by the evangelists on the lips of the dying Jesus: "*My God, my God, why have you forsaken me?*" Here again we find a tangle of contrasting prophecies that only the Christians' Messiah seems to fulfil: "*But I am a worm, and no man, the scorn of mankind, the laughing-stock of the nations. All who see me mock me, sneering and wagging their heads.*" So it begins.

It rises in a crescendo; but this is followed by a sudden transition from the utmost humiliation to the utmost glory: "*All the ends of the earth will remember and return to the Lord. All the descendants of the nations will bow down before him, for dominion belongs to the Lord and he reigns over all nations. All the great ones on earth will bow low before him. ... All my children will serve him and will tell of him to generation after generation. ...*"

For the believer, these prophecies of intermingled victory and defeat have been fulfilled not only in the earthly life of Jesus himself but also in what the course of history has meted out to his message. Christian theology asserts that the churches are Jesus himself through the ages, and they too have met with both defeat and victory.

Side by side with betrayals and infamies committed down the centuries by people professing to be Christians there have been shining examples of heroism, personal sacrifice and boundless love to the bitter end. So the prophecy seems to have been fulfilled not only in Christ but also in the history of Christianity: all that is most base and most sublime, most infamous and most heroic, is intertwined – just as defeat and victory are intertwined in the ancient prophecies.

A Messiah who upsets all expectations

'The gospel-writers built up a Messiah to fit in with their own expectations. The characteristics they attributed to him were those that the prophecies required. Jesus is a prefabricated construction, put together bit by bit like a mosaic to incorporate all the Old Testament prophecies.'

Assertions such as these have been made by numerous scholars who have concerned themselves with the origins of Christianity. In the chapters that follow we intend to make a detailed examination of the reasons which lead us to consider their suspicions groundless.

For the time being we will simply make a few comments relevant to the Christian conviction that Jesus alone is the 'decipherment key' to the Hebrew scriptures.

Here is what has been written by one of the foremost biblical scholars of our time, Père Lagrange (admittedly he is a believer, but what he says is borne out by historical fact):

'Belief in Christ, Son of God and redeemer of mankind, cannot arise out of the Judaism of the Pharisees or the old scriptural writings by way of literal interpretation only. No attempt at bringing together all the messianic prophecies and drawing from them an anticipatory portrait of Jesus could possibly succeed. Christianity did not emerge from the old Revelation through a process of purely rational interpretation. So long as St Paul interpreted the Old Testament by himself, as a Pharisee, he remained a Pharisee.'

And we might add that so long as Italo Zolli studied the scriptures as a Jew, he remained Chief Rabbi of Rome.

The fact is that Jesus is a Messiah who upset all the mental images and preconceptions current in the old Israel. For Judaism the messianic figure was (and still is) the object of contrasting expectations. It could hardly be otherwise, given the number of contradictory traits the prophecies attribute to 'the one who is to come'.

But there is no doubt that alongside the conviction that an enigmatic personage sprung from their own race would have an impact world-wide, the Jews (and not only Jesus's contemporaries) envisaged a messianic 'kingdom' in the full sense of the word – a powerful earthly kingdom which would make Israel the governor and master of many nations. According to Epstein: 'the references to the Messiah throughout the Hebrew prophecies are essentially concerned with a terrestrial future. And the blissful future promised by the prophecies was not thought of in a religious context only.'

Moreover history confirms that this was indeed the generally held expectation: innumerable pseudo-messiahs sprang up within Judaism, and each one of them tried to head a movement that was both religious and politico-military. And each time everything ended in tragedy. We shall look in a later chapter at a few of the ones who in Jesus's own day showed what was typically expected of the Messiah. The New Testament itself is full of the impatience of the crowds, and even of the disciples, who wanted to set up a magnificent kingdom by the power of the sword; and it makes no secret of the disappointment felt by some with this Messiah who forbade even self-defence, who counselled prudence in order not to stir up patriotic fervour, and who chose a way to glory that passed through humiliation and suffering.

Of all Israel's messiahs, Jesus is the only one to have achieved success – although he chose the way to failure, humanly speaking. He is the only one to have overcome the old Israel's inability to distinguish between religious history and political history. He is *'the chosen one of Yahweh'* who (as Isaiah prophesies in chapter 42) *'will not cry out or raise his voice'* as *'he brings justice to the nations'.* Yet in their numberless interpretations of the messianic texts, the Jews expected 'Someone' who would be at one and the same time both earthly king and high priest. The general expectation therefore ran along lines quite contrary to the course followed by Jesus. For believers he is the only valid 'key' to the messianic enigma – the one awaited by Isaiah who *'will steadfastly bring forth justice'* without *'breaking the bruised reed or snuffing out the smoking wick'.* The possibility of his having been thought up by devout Jews as a myth does seem remote, for a cultural development of that sort would have been inexplicable against that background and amidst those expectations.

More will be said about this in due course.

Jesus is not only the one who seems to provide the key to the enigma of 'a man of sorrows' who at the same time attains to the glory of kingship.

The kingship he chose for himself is the only one that can genuinely claim to 'inscribe its laws in the hearts of men for ever' – as the prophecies so often proclaimed.

Great empires pass away. Egypt, Babylon and Rome ended in ruins.

In the twenty centuries since the appearance of this Messiah, his reign has shown itself to be the only one that can have no end. Why so?

A king for both hearts and heads

The scriptures foretold the coming of a king. For those who believe in the Christ of the gospels the one who came was the most magnificent of all possible kings.

'With what great pomp and splendour he came, in the eyes of hearts that appreciate wisdom', reflected Pascal as he remarked that there are three ways of 'reigning'.

There is the greatness of monarchs, leaders, politicians: they dominate nations by force or by innate ability, often with bloodshed and deception.

Then there is a second type of greatness: the one grounded on wisdom and intellectual prowess. It is the greatness of the geniuses 'who have their own power and glory, their own victories. And they need none of that material grandeur which means nothing to them. They stand out not because of their appearance but because of their brains. And that is all they want.'

Yet there is a third, far higher, way of 'reigning', a third type of greatness. It is that of the dimension in which, from what we are told of him, Jesus chose to live and die. The eye of faith sees in him the one promised by God as described by Isaiah, again in chapter 42: *"I have formed you and made you a covenant for the people, a light for the nations, so that you may open the eyes of the blind and free the prisoners from the dungeons, those who dwell in darkness from their prison."* His reign is the one in which love, humility, poverty and service prevail.

It is in this last order of greatness that the Christians' Messiah is unsurpassably king. Believers accept this Messiah because in him they perceive the perfect realisation of the Old Testament prophecies. No other king could have brought such fulfilment of the promises. The king who did come was the only one whose dominion is worthy of acceptance by the hearts and minds of men of all times and all places. As the prophet Daniel put it: *'the God of heaven will set up a kingdom which will never be destroyed, and its sovereignty will never pass to another people'* (chapter 2).

Apropos the difficulty so many Jews find in accepting the Christians' Messiah, Pascal remarks: 'They say: "Jesus got killed; he had to submit; he did not subjugate the pagans; he did not bring us the spoils of victory, nor did he bring us riches." Is that all they can say? It is precisely because of all this that I find him worthy of my love. I really would not wish for the one whom they would have liked to see come.'

His words have not passed away

In chapter 24 of the gospel according to Matthew there is a striking saying attributed to Jesus: *"Heaven and earth will pass away, but my words will never pass away."*

Until now we have been looking at the Jewish scriptures to see whether their prophecies reached some sort of objective fulfilment in what is recorded in the Christian scriptures and in subsequent history. The only New Testament prediction we propose to test is the one contained in that saying attributed to Jesus by Matthew.

Benedetto Croce (a philosopher whom nobody can possibly suspect of engaging in Christian apologetics) once wrote: 'Christianity is the greatest revolution that humanity has ever achieved.' He went on to demonstrate – with all the rigour of a historian deaf to every religion except that of simple human freedom – that Jesus's message has been ever-present and ever-alive in all the idealistic movements that have arisen since that message was first delivered nearly twenty centuries ago. Even in movements that have nothing whatever to do with the Church or with churches. One of Croce's best-known sayings is: 'For this reason we cannot avoid calling ourselves Christians.'

At much the same time Paul Louis Couchoud – a brilliant 'demolisher' of the historicity of Jesus whom we shall be quoting quite often – wrote the following (in justification of his attempt to destroy the historical foundations of Christianity): 'Within men's minds, within that ideal world that exists under the skull, Jesus is immeasurable, limitless. His proportions are beyond compare, his order of greatness barely conceivable. The whole history of the western world from the Roman empire on is governed by one central fact, one generative phenomenon: the collective making-present of Jesus and of his death. Everything else has either sprung from that or adapted itself to that. All that has been done in the west in the course of many centuries has been done in the enormous shadow cast by the cross.'

It was the thought of that cross that made Renan say: 'To wrench the name of Jesus out of the world would be to shake the world's very foundations.'

Here we have statements of objective historical fact, fact that is undeniable. And they are made by people like Couchoud and Renan, who took it upon themselves to 'unmask the Christian misunderstanding' precisely because of its immense importance. And yet on the same plane of objectivity, the historical reality of this Jesus who has done such violence to history – becoming for Hegel history's 'pivot', for Nietzsche its 'supreme turning-point' and for Couchoud 'the invisible master who governs the human race' – is no more than a fleeting dot. From a barely visible single seed a vast forest has grown, with an exuberance that seems to defy explanation.

The voice of history is a voice that carries conviction; and it brooks no argument. There is now general agreement that first the French revolution and then the Marxist movement are explicable historically only as post-Christian phenomena.

Engels recognised that scientific socialism, Marxism, draws on Christianity and its Hebrew sources for its own thirst for justice and love for mankind, for its concept of the person as well as its ideas about social conflict and about history as progress. The old religious message has been secularised, as we shall see better later.

Similarly the 'Liberty, Equality, Fraternity' of the French revolutionaries was a gospel slogan. And few historians would deny that the emergence of the present-day entrepreneurial bourgeoisie can be explained by the way in which Protestantism understood and lived its Christianity.

What does all this add up to?

That the head-on collision between socialism and liberalism which characterises our times has roots that go down to the preaching recorded by the author of Matthew's gospel.

It is just one of many examples of that invincible tenacity and endurance.

His words have not passed away.

5.

. . . in the fulness of time

But in the fulness of time God sent his own Son, born of woman, born under the Law, to redeem those who were under the Law, so that we might receive adoption as sons.

GALATIANS 4, 4–5

How glad one is to find a little light amid so much darkness! How good it is to see, with the eye of faith, Darius and Cyrus, Alexander, the Romans, Pompey and Herod all unwittingly contributing to the glory of the Gospel!

BLAISE PASCAL

A treasure-hunt full of pitfalls

The prophetic writings are a fascinating area to explore but they can be as perilous as quicksands. So, as we now venture into them a little further we shall maintain a firmer foothold than ever on historical facts that are as far as possible indisputable. The question this chapter is going to ask is one that has to be answered with the greatest possible prudence.

Is it possible to trust those who declare that biblical prophecy went as far as specifying the date of the beginning of the messianic era?

Consequently, was there a valid prediction of the date for the appearance of the One whom Christians were to acknowledge as the Christ foretold by the prophets?

We have no time for, or interest in, esoteric interpretations. We are quite certain that the Bible is no sort of enciphered calendar designed for dabblers in occult divination of one kind or another.

But we do believe that, with due caution, reason can venture at least some distance in this treasure-hunt to which the hidden God seems to invite us.

So let us go a little further and search for more precise pointers than we have found so far.

Flavius Josephus and his 'ambiguous prophecy'

Flavius Josephus was a Jew of the priestly caste who went over to the Roman side after having played a leading part in the Jewish insurrection of AD 66–70 which culminated in the destruction of Jerusalem, the temple and the whole of Israel. In his celebrated *'Jewish War'* (written in Greek) Josephus described events of which he had first-hand knowledge. His book is the most important document we have on first-century Israel.

This Jewish historian describes the quite remarkable emergence of a number of false messiahs, all prompted by the conviction that 'the time had come'.

In chapter 5 of the 6th book of his history he makes one rather surprising statement: *'But what most incited* (the Jews) *to make war was an ambiguous prophecy, also found in holy scripture, according to which "one from their country would at that time become master of the world".'*

Josephus hastens to give his own interpretation of the prophecy – which he had every interest in declaring ambiguous: that same interpretation had saved his life when, having gone over to the Romans, he was taken before their commander Vespasian (in deference to whom he took unto himself the name of Flavius).

'*This* (the 'ambiguous prophecy') *was understood by the Jews to apply to one of their own race, so very many of them misinterpreted it; in fact the prophecy referred to the mastery of Vespasian, who was acclaimed emperor while he was in Judaea.'*

Leaving aside the differing interpretations, we nonetheless have here good evidence that first-century Israel took it for granted that *'at that time'* the *'master of the world'* would arise in Judaea.

Although Josephus declared the prophecy 'ambiguous' in order to apply it to the new ruler, for the great mass of Jews it must have been the reverse of ambiguous since (according to Josephus himself) it was their major incitement to defiance of the greatest military power in the world. Wasn't the master of all the nations due to appear at that very time? Under his leadership the Jews would not only conquer in battle but also completely overthrow the great empire of Rome whose very name struck terror into the hearts of all nations. That was the hope that inspired the defenders of Jerusalem to prefer death to acceptance of the repeated peace overtures made by the besiegers.

'All the times have come and gone'

That this expectation of a 'master of the world' should have taken such a hold on an entire people, and overcome even fear of death, may well surprise those of us who know how things turned out.

But why did Israel await its Messiah at the very time that Jesus – whom the whole Roman empire was later to acknowledge as the Christ – appeared? Why in the first century and not in a past or future century in the long religious history of Judaism?

Two particular passages in scripture seem likely to have been the sources from which the Jews deduced a date, albeit approximate, for the coming of 'the Anointed One'. Their interpretation of those passages is of course the one adopted by Christians, in whose view the Messiah certainly did come at the time the Jews were expecting him. We shall be looking at those texts a little later.

That century brought conviction and certainty to the

adherents of the new faith that sprang from Jesus; but it brought disillusionment and disappointment to those of the Jews who could not bring themselves to acknowledge any of the many candidates for messiahship that the age produced. There is excellent evidence that this disappointment caused the teachers of Israel to alter little by little the interpretations which had led their forbears to single out the first century for the long-awaited coming. Since 'all the times have come and gone', as the Talmud itself says (Sanhedrin 97), some explanation for the disappointed hope needed to be found.

Some Jewish scholars now see messianism as an abstract idea – the idea of personal and collective human longing for history to be shaped by religion and justice, the idea that human endeavour must eventually bring about a dawn of redemption in which evil will no longer hold sway.

All the same, it is a matter of indisputable historical fact that during the first century – the century of Jesus himself – the situation was as Paul described it: *'Pagans who were not seeking righteousness found it through faith; whereas Israel, looking for a righteousness deriving from law, failed to carry out the law's requirements'* (Romans 9).

In saying this we are certainly not making any value judgment. We are interested only in establishing the facts, and they are these: on the historical plane Israel's expectation of a Messiah built up to a climax, and then decreased (or, rather, the content of the expectation changed) just when the pagan world was accepting a Messiah whom it had never expected. And while the new faith began to expand, Judaism turned back on itself in an attempt to explain the non-arrival of the Christ it had been awaiting for so long.

How does 'official' Judaism nowadays see the matter? One view now frequently encountered is that 'we were mistaken; the Messiah is not still to come for he comes all the time. The Christ foretold by the prophets is not a person, as we thought for so many centuries. The Christ is ourselves, the people of Israel.' Thus Isaiah's moving predictions concerning the 'suffering servant of Yahweh' are to be applied to the Jewish people as a whole. No Jewish scholar will contest their messianic character, but he will prefer to say that they refer not to any individual but rather to the Jewish race, which by the example of its sufferings endured in unfailing fidelity to the Everlasting One will bring all men to acknowledge the Lord.

But this new interpretation does more than forget the old tradition. It also fails to tally with Isaiah in places where the text makes a clear distinction between the person of the Messiah and the Jewish people as a whole. For instance, in chapter 49 (6) the mysterious personage is seen as restoring and leading his people, and in 53 (4–6) as being alone in paying the price of his people's sins. And in 53 (8–9) it is said that he will be *'stricken for the transgressions of the people'*, *'killed and buried'*. There is difficulty in making this apply to the whole people envisaged by the 'collectivity' theory arrived at by Jewish exegetes of today.

We have no king but Caesar

As we said earlier, two scriptural passages in particular seem likely to have been the data for the calculations that led the Jews to defy Rome and expose their land to the worst Rome could do.

The first is the one in chapter 49 of Genesis in which Jacob blesses his sons and says: *"Gather round, because I want to tell you what will befall you in the last days."* ('The last days' is the expression commonly used in the Bible to denote the new age to be inaugurated by the Messiah.) *"The sceptre shall not be taken from Judah, nor the mace from between his feet, until the coming of Him to whom it belongs, and to Him shall go the obedience of the nations."*

We have it on good authority that Jewish exegetes have always read this passage in a messianic sense.

Now, history shows that 'the sceptre was taken away from Judah, and the mace from between his feet' just at the time when Jesus made his appearance. Herod the Great (the one alleged to have ordered 'the slaughter of the innocents') was the last king of the Jews. On his death the land of Israel was divided up, all authority passed into the hands of Roman governors and even the semblance of Jewish autonomy came to an end. From then until the end of the British Mandate in 1948 the Jews ceased to be masters in the land of their fathers.

When Pontius Pilate asked those who wanted Jesus condemned: *"Am I to crucify your king?"*, the gospel of John records the reply: *"We have no king but Caesar."* This is not the place for discussing whether or not those words were in fact spoken. The point is that they reflect a precise, objective historical situation. And they impress the Christian, for he sees them confirming the political situation foretold for the messianic era and put in writing more than a thousand years earlier.

In his notes for his *Apologia for Christianity*, Pascal twice commented on them thus: 'Therefore Jesus was the Messiah, because the Jews had no king except a foreigner and did not want any others.'

That is of course a Christian comment. But there is no doubt that Roman domination and the end of independence (soon to be followed by the end of the state of Israel) were seen by the Jews of the time to be related to the prophecy attributed to Jacob. And this quickened expectation of the coming of the Messiah.

The book of Daniel

However, in Jesus's time attention was concentrated above all on the book attributed to Daniel. Present-day archaeological discoveries have, as we shall see, provided fresh confirmation of this.

Daniel is the last and richest expression of messianic

prophecy in the Old Testament. Even Renan considered that 'the book of Daniel gives supreme and definitive expression to the messianic hope'.

The text progresses steadily towards the Great Prophecy contained in chapter 9. It is here that one can, it is said, find the one and only indication in scripture of the date of the Messiah's coming; not surprisingly – given the genre, and the fact that God is a hidden God – it is less than self-evident.

For our purposes it does not matter whether the book was written during the exile in Babylonia in the sixth century BC (as was thought by most exegetes for a considerable time) or whether earlier traditions were drawn on for its composition much later, around 160 BC (as later research reliably suggests).

What is perfectly certain, and amply proved by discoveries of papyrus scrolls, is that by Jesus's time the book of Daniel had been written and read in its present form for close on two centuries. That is all that matters for our purposes.

A small stone grows into a great mountain

The first messianic allegory in Daniel occurs in the second chapter: a small stone breaks and topples the great composite statue symbolising the four empires that were to precede the coming of the Christ. According to one interpretation these four empires were those of the Babylonians, the Medes, the Persians and the Greeks, pictured by the writer as four metals – gold, silver, bronze and iron mixed with clay. Another interpretation classes the Medes along with the Persians and identifies the fourth empire as that of the Romans.

Which of the two interpretations is correct does not concern us; we are more interested in how the text proceeds:

'The stone that had struck the statue became a great mountain that filled the whole earth.' This means, adds the prophet, that *"the God of heaven will set up a kingdom*

which will never be destroyed, and its sovereignty will never pass to another people. It will break in pieces all these kingdoms and bring them to an end, but as for itself it will endure for ever. The great God has made known to the king what is to happen in the future. The dream is certain and its interpretation sure."

Thus the messianic kingdom, the one that 'will never be destroyed' and 'will endure for ever', is at first likened to a small stone. But that small stone is not only strong enough to destroy every earthly empire; it grows into 'a great mountain that fills the whole earth'.

History shows this to be typical of the messianic reign inaugurated by Jesus. There was no sudden explosion of strength, no great display of power from the very start. But there was 'a little stone' which took several centuries to grow into 'a great mountain'. *'The kingdom of heaven is like a grain of mustard-seed'*, say the gospel-writers.

The son of man

The prophecy becomes more precise in chapter 7, with Daniel's own dream and visions:

'And behold, coming on the clouds of heaven I saw one like a son of man. He came to the Ancient of Days and was led into his presence. To him were given dominion, honour and sovereignty, and men of all peoples, nations and languages served him. His dominion is an eternal dominion that will never pass away, and his sovereignty is such as will never be destroyed.'

In the gospels Jesus himself often alludes to this passage from Daniel, calling himself 'the son of man' and thus relating his coming to that prophecy. This is especially noticeable in Matthew's gospel where the expression occurs nearly thirty times.

As the term 'son of man' occurs only once in the Old Testament, in the passage from Daniel just cited, its use by the gospel-writers does amount to a direct appeal to that prophecy of Daniel. The fact that Matthew's gospel, which reflects Christian teaching to Jews, uses it so often shows not only that the messianic hope of the ordinary people owed a great deal to this particular prophecy but also that the passage itself was generally understood by Jews in a messianic sense.

The author of the book goes on to say that the citizens of this Kingdom 'which will never pass away' will be called *'saints of the Most High'*, and that *'the kingdom will be theirs for ever, for ever and ever'*.

We have noted how Renan remarked that in Daniel's vision Israel's messianic hope reached supreme and definitive expression. From then on, he wrote, 'the Messiah ceased to be a king after the style of David and Solomon ... : he was a Son of man who was to appear on a cloud, a supernatural being though human in appearance, entrusted with power to judge the whole world and preside over the golden age'.

If the textual critics are correct in saying that the book of Daniel was written very late – not until about 160 BC – this dating tends to bear out what thoughtful believers have always held concerning the 'history of salvation' – i.e. that it is a long, slow progress, spanning many centuries, from vague and indistinct promises to a messianic hope that gradually becomes more precise until in the very late book of Daniel it reaches definitive expression.

So it is hardly surprising that we now find prophecy going as far as to give an indication of the date at which the predictions will be fulfilled.

The seventy weeks

The prophecy of the 'seventy weeks' occurs in the ninth chapter of the book of Daniel:

'Seventy weeks are decreed concerning your people and the holy city, to put an end to transgression, to seal off sin, to

atone for iniquity, to bring about everlasting righteousness, to set the seal on both vision and prophet and to anoint the Holy of Holies.'

So, for the prophet, the new era – when all sin is expiated and everlasting justice reigns supreme – will begin when the Christ is anointed. And then there will be no more prophetic visions.

All this will happen after 'seventy weeks'. There has never been much argument about the meaning of this expression: clearly it is not a question of weeks but of *periods of seven years;* so the 'seventy weeks' are 70 times 7 years – 490 years in all.

But at what point in time should one begin the count? There is a clue in what follows in the biblical text: the count should begin from 'the word to return and rebuild Jerusalem'.

But which 'word', which decree?

Some have said that it was the decree of Artaxerxes in the seventh year of his reign, i.e. in 458–457 BC. Starting from that date the 490 years would come to an end in AD 32–33.

Others have maintained that it was the decree of Cyrus, in the year 538, marking Israel's liberation from exile in Babylonia. The 490 years would then end in 48 BC. Although it is now certain that Jesus was in fact born several years before the traditional date of his birth, there is here an 'error' of about forty years.

The first interpretation would have seemed the more likely, given that the prophecy appears to allude to the killing of the Messiah, for which AD 32–33 is a highly likely date.

There really does seem to be something quite out of the ordinary about the fact that the one and only instance – in the whole lengthy prophetic tradition – of prediction of a date should be capable of giving one date that in fact did usher in (at least for Christians) the start of the messianic era. Even a discrepancy of seventy years seems little enough after so many centuries of waiting.

It is also noteworthy that this prophecy speaks of *'an Anointed one'* – that is to say a Messiah, a Christ – *'who will be suppressed'*, and goes on to refer to *'the people of the prince who will come and destroy the city and the sanctuary'*. Jerusalem and its temple were in fact destroyed by Titus, the Roman emperor, in the year AD 70.

All the same it must be said that these verses can be interpreted quite differently. It is perfectly possible to see in Daniel not predictions of Jesus and Titus but references to the high priest Onias III and Antiochus. In all this let us go on seeking facts and facts only. Nonetheless we are surely entitled to be impressed when we find, immediately after the prophecy of the date of the messianic era, predictions which – even if they are open to other interpretations – do seem applicable to the period in history immediately following Jesus. And the fall of Jerusalem in AD 70 has always been held by reputed Jewish exegetes to mark the end of Daniel's 'seventy weeks'.

Qumran and the Essenes

In recent years fresh light has been thrown on the whole matter by the accidental discovery by a bedouin shepherd of the Qumran manuscripts, the Dead Sea Scrolls. In Jesus's day, Qumran was the main centre of a Jewish sect called the Essenes about whom little was known until the discovery of their documents in 1947. These had been hidden in a barely accessible cave when the community fled before the Romans, probably between AD 66 and 70.

The scrolls contain the texts of almost all the books of the Hebrew bible; copied out one or two centuries before Jesus, they nonetheless tally perfectly with the texts used by Jews and Christians to this day. Moreover the scrolls also disclose the whole of Essene teaching, which it is now possible to compare with that of Jesus; we shall deal with this aspect of the discovery later.

For the time being let us take a brief look at what the Dead Sea Scrolls can contribute to interpretation of the prophecies.

They have shown that the Essenes – a Jewish élite living according to a strict rule, and much given to reading the signs of the times that were to herald the coming of the Messiah – set great store by Daniel's 'seventy weeks'.

What is more, the scrolls lend some support to the second of the two 'calculations' concerning the beginning of the 490 years, i.e. the one that would take Cyrus's decree of 538 BC as starting-point. But with two important differences. The Essenes based their calculation not on the end but the beginning of the Babylonian exile, in 586; and then they subtracted the seventy years of exile before subtracting the 490 years. This resulted in their expecting the messianic era to begin in 26 BC; and it also effectively reduced Daniel's 'error' from forty years to twenty.

Since the Essenes and their interpretations of scripture were held in high esteem in the Jewish world, and since there are good grounds for thinking that other Jewish schools of thought made calculations along the same lines, we can begin to understand why expectation of the Messiah's coming had reached such a pitch by Jesus's time.

There is archaeological evidence as well for this. Excavations at Qumran have shown that new buildings were erected there not long before 26 BC. And coins found during the same excavations confirm that the community was fully organised and intensely active from about 20 BC until AD 70. The buildings were extended so as to accommodate the growing number of those who sought to retire to the desert to await the Messiah. The Essene *Manual of Discipline*, also discovered in the cave, lays down that: 'At that time men will have to stop living in the corrupt world and withdraw to the desert, where those who are to hold themselves in readiness in those days must receive instruction.' 'Those days' are the time of the long-awaited Messiah's appearance.

It is not difficult to see why Jesus was able to announce at the start of his ministry: *"The time is ripe; the Kingdom of Heaven is at hand."*

Non-Jewish expectation

That the Jews should have been expecting their mysterious Christ at just that time is remarkable enough.

But what is even more remarkable is that other nations too were living in a state of expectancy at that same time. There is indisputable evidence of wellnigh universal waiting for 'Someone' who was to come out of Judaea.

From both Tacitus and Suetonius, two of the greatest Roman historians, we learn that the nations were in ferment at the approach of what we now call the first century AD.

Tacitus, *Annals:* 'Most of them were convinced that the ancient writings of the priests provided evidence that at about this time the East would gain the upper hand, and that the masters of the world would come from Judaea.'

Suetonius, *Life of Vespasian:* 'Throughout the East there was a steady spread of the old idea that it was part of the world's destiny that the masters of the world would come from Judaea at that time.'

Both these historians were writing in roughly AD 100, when in the poorer districts of many Mediterranean cities Christians were already worshipping the one from Judaea who was indeed to become the 'master' of the western world. But neither Tacitus nor Suetonius realised the historical significance of Christian preaching, even if they knew anything at all about it (and it is by no means certain that they did). The triumph of 'the king from Judaea' was then still to come, and the two historians thought they were discussing an event still awaited, not one that had already occurred.

But there is more still to be said. We now know for certain

that the most celebrated astrologers of the ancient world, those of Babylon, not only expected the Palestinian Messiah but had predicted the date of his coming with even more exactitude than the Essenes. Here are the facts; draw from them what conclusions you think fit.

The enigma of a star over Bethlehem

Matthew's gospel recounts that a *star* (the text never speaks of a *comet*) shone in the sky above Bethlehem when Jesus was born, and that subsequently some 'wise men' from the East arrived there.

We shall never know for certain whether these things really happened. But the theory that Matthew's account was purely symbolical certainly ought to take stock of what has been discovered in the course of the last three hundred years.

There now appears to be scientific proof that the Babylonian astrologers (almost certainly Matthew's 'wise men') awaited the birth of 'the master of the world' in 7 BC. Along with 6 BC, 7 BC is considered by modern scholars to be among the most probable dates of Jesus's birth.

In light of this, can one entirely discount those two verses in the second chapter of Matthew? '*When Jesus was born in Bethlehem of Judaea in the days of king Herod, behold, wise men from the East came to Jerusalem saying: "Where is he who has been born king of the Jews? For we have seen his star in the East and have come to worship him".*'

Here is an outline of what has finally led to some understanding of why 'wise men from the East' should have arrived in Jerusalem with their awkward question. It reads rather like a detective story.

In December 1603, in Prague, Johannes Kepler (one of the fathers of modern astronomy) observed the brilliant conjunction of Jupiter and Saturn within the constellation of the Fishes (Pisces). Kepler made a number of calculations and concluded that the same phenomenon must have occurred in 7 BC. He later discovered a very old commentary on the scriptures by Rabbi Arbanel which recalled that, according to one Jewish belief, the Messiah would appear precisely at the time when Jupiter and Saturn came together in the constellation of Pisces.

Very few people attributed much importance to Kepler's discoveries, principally because textual criticism was then a long way from establishing that Jesus was in fact born earlier than the traditional date. So 7 BC rang no bells. Moreover Kepler was a little too inclined to add mystical speculation to scientific fact.

More than two centuries later the Danish scholar Münter discovered and deciphered a medieval Jewish commentary on the 'seventy weeks' of Daniel. Münter was then able to show that in the Middle Ages too the conjunction of Jupiter and Saturn in the constellation of Pisces was, for some learned Jews, one of the signs that would accompany the birth of the Messiah.

The contents of an Egyptian papyrus now preserved in Berlin were published in 1902. This document records all the movements of the planets from 17 BC to AD 10 and confirms Kepler's calculation concerning 7 BC. The conjunction of Jupiter and Saturn was indeed observed in that year and was brilliantly visible all over the Mediterranean. Nor do modern astronomers dispute Kepler's calculation.

Finally, in 1925 the *Stellar calendar of Sippar* was published. This is a terracotta tablet with cuneiform writing from the ancient city of Sippar on the Euphrates, site of an important school of Babylonian astrology. The calendar records all the movements and conjunctions for the year 7 BC. Why this particular year? Because according to the Babylonian astrologers the conjunction of Jupiter and Saturn in the constellation of Pisces was then due to occur three times: on 29 May, 1 October and 5 December. The conjunction normally occurs every 794 years, but only once; whereas in 7 BC it occurred three times. Modern astronomers do not dispute these calculations by the ancient experts in Sippar.

Archaeologists have at last uncovered the meaning of the Babylonian astrologers' symbology. Jupiter was the planet of the masters of the world, Saturn the planet 'protector' of Israel. The constellation of Pisces was the sign of 'the end of the times', i.e. the beginning of the messianic era.

So, might there not be something more than myth behind Matthew's account of the arrival in Jerusalem from the East of wise men asking *"Where is he who has been born king of the Jews?"*

One thing that *is* certain is that between the Tigris and the Euphrates, as in the whole of the East, people not only awaited a Messiah who would come from Israel but had also decided – with quite astounding assurance – that he would be born at a specific time.

And it was the time at which, in the Christian view, the 'master of the world' did indeed make his appearance.

'The hour has come'

Thus there was a concentration of attention, a build-up of expectation, around the years of Jesus's earthly life.

The people of Israel were facing the end of their political independence and thinking about Jacob's prediction that the Christ would come just before 'the sceptre would be taken away from Judah'.

The Essenes were appealing to people to join them in the desert so as to await in prayer and penitence the One who was to come. And they were not far out in their prediction of the date.

In the plains of Mesopotamia astronomers and astrologers were agreed in deciding that a Messiah would come from Judaea to rule the world, and they had decided that his reign would begin in the year that was later called, incorrectly, the seventh before Christ.

In the poorer districts of the Roman empire's cities there was ferment; even among the pagans expectation was lively – and it was centred on Israel. The excitement was great enough for major Roman historians to think it worth a mention in their works.

We therefore have here a well-documented historical fact: in the first century the world's attention was concentrated on that distant province of the Roman empire. And there, belief in the prophecies and trust in the explanations of them given by the scholars were strong enough to inspire the people to revolt against the Romans. 'Masters of the world' for only a little while longer, thought the rebels, for the one who was to master even the all-powerful empire was about to come.

History therefore seems to bear witness in an obscure way to the saying the evangelists attribute to Jesus: *"The time is ripe, the hour of salvation has come."*

Human history appears to pause for a moment for breath as it awaits what is to come. While the star shines over Palestine Augustus gives the world one of the few periods of peace that history has recorded. The gates of the temple of Janus, the god of the armies, are closed: the 'pax romana' has been declared.

On the other hand it has been suggested that this waiting, this general expectancy, may have tipped the scales in Jesus's favour. Wasn't the ground admirably suited to the germination of his cult? Whether the origin of Christianity lay in a man gradually divinised by faith or in a myth gradually humanised to coincide with a man called Jesus is of no importance: the new faith could very easily have spread simply as a consequence of all these favourable circumstances. Thus a number of people argue.

We shall examine this theory more fully later. For the time being we wish merely to draw attention to one more objective fact for which there is ample documentation, i.e.

the fate of Israel's religious pre-eminence after 'all the times had come and gone' without the appearance of a Messiah whom all Jews would recognise.

Israel's 'before' and 'after'

Within Israel's long religious history spanning thousands of years it is easy to discern a clear-cut division – a 'before' and an 'after'.

Production of writings considered to be inspired by Yahweh himself ceased about one hundred years before Jesus appeared. By about 100 BC the Old Testament as we have it today was generally recognised as 'normative', and in the first century AD the Jewish religious authorities definitively fixed the canon of the twenty-four books of their Bible.

Thus within the space of about 200 years a number of decisive events occurred. No more additions to Holy Scripture were henceforth possible. The one whom part of the world was to acknowledge as the Messiah foretold by the prophets duly made his appearance. The temple of Jerusalem was destroyed once and for all; priesthood and sacrifice came to an end. The Jewish dispersion (diaspora) throughout the world reached massive proportions. Within Palestine Judaism was reduced to a mere flicker as the result of the revolt of AD 70.

There were to be no more prophets of scriptural status. Israel's religious creativity seemed to die away, to be replaced by interpretative study and commentary. Judaism certainly remained as the sole survivor of the ancient world's religions, but its missionary strength seemed exhausted and, by contrast with former days, it was henceforth to achieve no expansion beyond the confines of its own race.

Israel's creativity died away on the very plane on which it had previously outstripped that of all its contemporaries – the religious plane. From the first century on, Judaism fell into decline – if 'decline' is the right word to describe the way it restricted itself to commenting on a religious inheritance that was to develop no further. There were indeed to be treasures of juridical and ethical wisdom; but in the Talmud's commentary on the Law and the Prophets intellectual subtlety is accompanied by a narrowness of vision that is in sad contrast with the broad sweep of biblical prophecy. Once prophecy fades, legalism becomes faith's last refuge.

The new Jewish prophets

Yet Israel did not lose all her creative power, nor her ability to leave her imprint on history. Although in the field of religion she became no more than the custodian of her beliefs, in other intellectual fields she remained – and still remains – a wonderfully alive and alert minority.

Marx, Freud, Einstein are but a few of the new Jewish prophets. They open up and lead the way into fresh territory – scientific socialism, depth psychology, the atomic era – but in what they have to tell the world there seems to be no longer any room for 'the new heaven'.

If Marx had lived in another age he might well have become a remarkable biblical prophet. But almost as if to give the coup de grâce to Israel's religious role in the world he directs all the messianic expectancy of his people towards his 'new earth':

'The working class is the true Messiah that will bring redemption to the world through its sufferings and its conflict with the sons of darkness, the bourgeoisie. Exploitation of the workers is the original sin. The socialist society of the future is the eschatological kingdom where the wolf will feed alongside the lamb and the earth will no longer bear thorns but fruit in abundance. The proletariat and the Party are the people of God on their way to this messianic kingdom. The factory is the house of prayer, and work is the new prayer. The leader of the proletariat is the prophet who shows the rest of Israel the way. Science is the true theology. ...'

How strange it can seem that this remarkable people's religious voice grew faint and weak just when the One whom it had foretold for centuries made his appearance.

And yet wasn't this too foretold in scripture? Is it not written in the book of Daniel that when the *'Holy of Holies'* is *'anointed'* the prophets and their predictions will come to an end: *'to set the seal on both vision and prophet'*?

6.

Three hypotheses

> *I have always found Thomas's prolonged doubt much more helpful than Mary Magdalen's unhesitating belief.*
>
> ST GREGORY THE GREAT

> *Christology suffers from a disease as yet incurable: psychological conjecture.*
>
> WILLIAM WREDE

There are three possible solutions

Jean Guitton has written: 'When I followed Albert Schweitzer's example and tried to list the various explanations offered as solutions to the Jesus problem, I was surprised to find how few there really were. I eventually came to the conclusion that in fact there are only three: two that are negative and one that is positive.'

Guitton calls these three possible solutions: (1) the 'critical', (2) the 'mythical' and (3) the answer of faith – the 'belief hypothesis'.

We too are of the opinion that the innumerable suggestions put forward to explain the enigma Jesus presents are in fact relatable to these three basic standpoints, even though individual authors within each school of thought may see the problem in a wide variety of ways. So we shall adopt Guitton's classification, though remaining aware of the dangers of over-simplification inherent in classification of any sort.

Quite early this century Schweitzer was able to say that, after three centuries of painstaking research, all the essential data were to hand for tackling systematically the problem posed by Jesus. If that was true then, it is all the more true now, after another period of intensive research enormously helped by what is called the 'archaeological revolution'. Thanks to the labours of many scholars, some of them believers but others not – historians, exegetes and archaeologists – we now have a mass of solidly-based but widely divergent conclusions for our thoughts to mull over.

Can we in fact bring them all back to the three basic positions discerned by Guitton?

But first of all what is meant by the 'critical' hypothesis (or solution, or school, or position) and the 'mythical' hypothesis? And where does faith, or belief, take its stand today?

The critical hypothesis: man into god

The *critical* hypothesis is the one advanced by many scholars who, having passed the New Testament through the sieve of what they call scientific criticism, do not deny that the central character of the drama did in fact exist as an historical figure. (Many such scholars therefore prefer their solution to be called 'historical' rather than 'critical'.)

Thus, the Christian faith had its origin in a man called Jesus. A quite exceptional man, certainly, but lacking any connection with the supernatural.

It is difficult to establish exactly what happened. The gospels are no help in this because they are documents of faith and not history.

What is certain is that after his death this elusive Jesus was divinised by his disciples, who attributed miracles to him and went as far as claiming that he rose from the dead.

Perhaps he was an itinerant preacher, like so many in Palestine in those days. Through a chain of unforeseeable circumstances it somehow befell him to be taken for the 'Son of God', even for God himself.

Perhaps he was a mad visionary who in the course of his

ravings called himself the Messiah awaited by the Jews; he was believed by a group of other visionaries, who in turn succeeded in convincing the rest of the world.

Perhaps his disciples were deluded, so bemuserd by the amazing ability of their master that they could not accept the fact that he had died and therefore declared him to have risen from the dead.

What criticism has to do is try to establish how much of what is recounted in the gospels is historical fact. But the starting-point has to be that it was the Church named after him that attributed divinity to Jesus. The gospels must therefore be stripped completely of every suggestion of the miraculous or the supernatural.

Jesus was no more than a man who was progressively divinised.

The Christ of faith is the final embellishment with which the community of believers adorned the Jesus of history.

Over his tomb (which either remained closed or else was found empty because somebody removed the body) the critical school of thought would inscribe the word 'IGNOTUS' – unknown, as Ricciotti has remarked.

The mythical hypothesis: god into man

The *mythical* (or *mythological*) school will have none of the historical existence of Jesus accepted by the critical school, stripped though that is of all supernatural elements. Instead it advances the hypothesis of the Jesus myth.

That is to say that Christianity had its origin not in any real man or any real events but in a legend, a myth. A very ancient myth, one that long pre-dated Christianity, of a god who becomes incarnate, suffers, dies and rises again to save mankind.

In some corner of the Roman empire a group of enthusiasts threw the mantle of this myth over the shoulders of someone they called Jesus. About him it is impossible to say anything with any historical certainty.

Or, even, this Jesus was a total invention – for the purpose of giving a name, a place and a life to the pre-existing myth of the god who conquers sin and death.

So there are really two mythical schools of thought, one moderate and one radical. The *moderates* do not go as far as totally denying the historical existence of the character in question, but they maintain that he himself – about whom nothing can possibly be known – does not matter. All that matters is the myth he incarnates. The *radicals* deny that any such man ever existed at all: Jesus is merely a name, invented in order to personify the legend.

Both moderates and radicals are agreed that what matters to scholars is not so much the history of Jesus as the myth of the Christ. According to the whole mythological school, some communities in antiquity quite simply transferred to him their belief in a sun myth (Dupuis), or the beliefs of Alexandrian allegory (Bauer), or an eastern cult of crucifixion as a liturgical act (Du Jardin). Or else Jesus is merely the Indian god Agni, or the Babylonian hero Gilgamesh or the Canaanites' sun-god in another guise.

In the opinion of Couchoud (to whom we shall refer quite often because he is one of the most brilliant and most radical exponents of this school of thought) the myth of a god who suffers and brings redemption was not put into words until after the year AD 100. At about that date it ceased to be simply visionary and lyrical and became written narrative: 'In one of the crowded districts of Rome at the end of the first century a pious stew was brewing, a sort of Christian hot-pot containing a bit of everything.' After coming to the boil all together in the pan, the ingredients of the myth got distilled in the first gospel. The life of Jesus recounted in this gospel is therefore 'nothing but an artificial legend – an imaginary account of events supposed to have taken place in Palestine about forty years before the destruction of

Jerusalem. The Jesus myth was weightily materialised.' (By this Couchoud means that the character in the legend, hitherto floating in the clouds of the imagination, was made to carry the weight of a detailed but completely fictitious 'history'.)

Whereas for the critical school of thought Christianity's origin lies in a man who got progressively divinised, for the mythical school *Jesus is a god who got progressively humanised.*

The Jesus of history is the final expression of belief in a Christ.

If the critical school would write IGNOTUS over his tomb, the mythological school would write NEMO – nobody.

One example: the loaves and fishes

The difference between the critical and mythological schools can best be illustrated by taking an example.

According to the evangelist John, Jesus satisfied the hunger of a crowd of about five thousand with five loaves and two fishes.

Critical interpretation: admittedly the episode was not a gospel-writer's addition but did convey what was remembered of some real happening; the crowd's hunger was indeed satisfied. But the bread and fish had been brought along beforehand; or else had been hidden away, to be brought out at a suitable moment. In the process of divinisation of the man Jesus, the primitive community's faith turned an unexpected distribution of food into a miracle. As with all the 'marvels' recounted in the gospels, we have here a perfectly normal happening blown up into something supernatural.

Mythical interpretation: no such distribution ever took place, nothing of the kind ever occurred, the loaves and fishes belong in the realm of myth. We have here one of the many legendary stories that go to make up the totally legendary set of writings known as the gospels. What scholars have to do is track down the myth that the community incarnated in this story which it circulated as historical fact.

Perhaps there was some harking back to the equally legendary Old Testament story about Moses who made manna come down from heaven. Or perhaps there is here an echo of some eastern mystery religion. Perhaps the explanation is to be found at psychological level: the idea of multiplication, latent within religious-minded man, was materialised and attributed to Jesus.

At odds with one another, but united in opposing the 'credulous believers'

The two *negative* solutions will be more clearly examined in later chapters. For the moment we would like simply to state that the fiercest of the battles have flared up not so much between 'believers' and 'sceptics' as between the two schools of thought among the latter.

Though united in denying anything of a transcendental nature to the origin of Christianity, the critical and mythical schools both accuse one another of making the emergence of the Christian faith incomprehensible. In the name of science and reason, scholars of both persuasions bandy acid reproaches of absurdity, self-contradiction and quite often bad faith.

The critical school, founded by the great eighteenth-century rationalists, registered its major successes in the nineteenth and early twentieth centuries; but it is now in decline (although its heirs still cling to its theories and publish best-sellers ...).

The more recent phenomenon – of better-informed scholars digging themselves into the mythological trench – is a result of the critical school's inability to give adequate answers to the questions *now* being posed in the name of reason – that same reason on which it prided itself in the first place.

We shall see this later. And we shall also see that the mythological school, although it appears to have the upper hand, is having to grapple with serious difficulties itself. Like the critical hypothesis before it, the mythical hypothesis has to reckon not only with the age-old objections but with the fresh facts brought to light by recent advanced study.

More and more agnostic and atheist scholars are frankly acknowledging that perhaps the wheel is coming full circle, and that in order to understand the origin of Christianity they will have to begin all over again.

Be that as it may, both schools are at one in levelling accusations of ingenuousness, outdatedness and lack of scientific spirit against those who persist in opting for the third of the possible solutions, the 'belief hypothesis', the answer of faith.

That is to say against those who call themselves believers because, having used their reasoning powers to the full, they admit (like Pascal) that the final step any rational man can take is to acknowledge that there are many, many things that transcend reason.

Against those 'credulous' believers who even now, faced with the enigma of Jesus and the origin of belief in him, still think that – all things considered – it is more rational to admit of a mysterious irruption of the divine into history at a certain point in time; who are not convinced, like the critical school, that the Christian faith makes an unwarranted incursion into the supernatural; who do not believe, like the mythologists, that the faith is based on a holy fable sprung from the fevered imagination of some middle-eastern maniacs.

A masked Christ

At the end of his study of the 'rationalist' interpretations of the origin of Christianity, G. Ricciotti wrote: 'One thing is obvious: acceptance of the portrait of Christ painted by the gospels or rejection of all or part of it are based more on philosophical than on historical criteria'.

This judgment is endorsed by no less a figure than Alfred Loisy, that revered master of the critical school, who wrote: 'If the christological problem that has fascinated thinkers and absorbed their attention for centuries is now being tackled afresh, this is less because the historical background is now better understood than because modern philosophy has been, and still is, experiencing a complete renewal.'

Not altogether surprisingly, given that they prefer philosophy to history, Loisy and a number of modern scholars often show a lack of interest in – even real distaste for – what archaeology brings to light; for them a commemorative stone tablet or a piece of papyrus are worth far less than their own individual theories. Such an attitude on the part of scholars who pride themselves on being 'scientific' seems paradoxical.[1]

Yet many examples of it can be given, and some will be given in later chapters. For the time being let us simply remark that the adjective 'scientific' so often applied to the innumerable theories about the origin of Christianity ought to be viewed with the utmost suspicion.

No one has any business to claim to reach truly scientific conclusions when the documents in themselves are judged insufficient for the construction of theories open to no attack. Loisy himself admitted that 'any history of the origins of Christianity is, willy nilly, like a house built on shaky foundations'. All that can possibly be constructed, given the available material, is a hypothesis: a *probable* rather than a *scientific* one. How many 'definitive' theories have had to be abandoned in the name of the 'science' that originally gave them birth. ... ?

Moreover it is very difficult to stay in the objective, impartial realm of science when one is tackling a subject that has innumerable historical, social, economic, political, even personal repercussions. What we know of Jesus touches us too closely for it not to have a profound effect on us. Complete neutrality in the study of a faith that for two thousand years has played a decisive role in world history is something that experience has shown to be beyond many people's capabilities.

Until now the 'history of the histories of Christ' has been for the most part a 'history of the philosophies about Christianity'. Every philosophical and cultural movement has eventually succeeded in conditioning the scholars of the period, so that they have mistaken the philosophical spirit of their age for scientific truth.

Christ has time and again been dressed up and given a mask to suit the fashion of the times.

In the days of the Enlightenment Jesus became an enlightened sage and teacher who preached about God and virtue. In the Romantics' day he was transformed into an astounding religious genius. In Kant's heyday he became the creator of an ethic, a moralist. Under the Nazis he became the prototype of the 'Aryan', in ill-fated conflict with the age-old 'Jewish conspiracy'. For Socialism and Communism he is at the head of a movement by the oppressed classes, a proletarian leader held captive and rendered harmless by the churches.

The preconceptions of the various brands of philosophy are, however, as nothing to some of the 'scientist' fictions presented to the public in all seriousness. Perhaps the ultimate was reached by Professor John Allegro's 'discovery' that *Jesus* is none other than the name of an hallucinatory fungus – a type of mushroom – used first in Mesopotamia and then by the Essenes; a remarkable mythologising process led to the Jesus-fungus being thought of as a Jesus-god; and from there it was but a short step to the idea of the god-man-Jesus – the obvious way for the drug-addicted devotees of the mushroom to 'actualise' their cult figure. ...

Historical or non-historical? What are the criteria?

There is a fundamental contradiction underlying much of textual criticism.

On the one hand, in order to show the utter absurdity and inanity of belief, the early Christian documents are declared completely devoid of historical value. The same demolition process is extended to cover even non-Christian material: every ancient text that is relevant is declared suspect, and very often rejected.

On the other hand, after firmly stating that we possess no really reliable documents on the origin of the faith, the critics set about picking and choosing among the individual verses of the New Testament texts: "This verse is reliable; this verse has certainly undergone elaboration; this one is undoubtedly a late interpolation."

But if all the documents one is working on are historically suspect, what criteria are adopted in this allegedly scientific picking and choosing?

Even E. Trocmé, an authoritative representative of the new scientific exegetical school, has pointed with some dismay to 'the incredible assurance with which people pass judgment on the authenticity, or lack of it, of the words attributed to Jesus by the gospels, although they have already stated that in this field one can be sure of nothing.'

If there is no evidence on which to build in order to establish what really happened, what is the yardstick for determining the reliability of this or that episode, this or that word or saying?

No satisfactory answer has ever been given to this question. 'One really must trust the specialists; after all, they are the ones who know their subject' (Trocmé). The plain truth is that no yardstick exists.

At least, each scholar devises his own, to suit his own ideological predilections and his own intellectual training.[2]

All the research into Jesus shows this to be the case.

To take just one example: in the name of 'scientific investigation' one author recognises that in the gospel accounts of the Passion there is a faint echo of an event that in fact took place; and he sets about 'proving' this, using his own pick-and-choose criteria. Outrage and scorn ensue among his peers who, on the basis of their own criteria, flatly deny the possibility of saying even that Jesus died by crucifixion and variously assert that he must have been strangled or stoned, or he died in a riot, or his disciples killed him, or he committed suicide, or the Romans beheaded him, or he died of old age after a fictitious death. Or else he never died at all, for the simple reason that he never so much as existed.

Moreover the lack of a reliable yardstick for determining what did happen is evident from the way individual specialists have shifted position. Why did Loisy at first 'prove' that only a madman could doubt the historicity of Paul's testimony, and later 'prove' that it would be 'extremely imprudent' to declare oneself sure either of Paul's testimony to the Jesus of history or of Paul's own real existence? Why, as the years went by, did he throw out as false hundreds of gospel verses that he had earlier declared to be authentic.

The answer is that he devised his own criteria, and progressively modified them to suit his own purposes.

Loisy once said of his opponents among the mythologists: 'The supposedly definitive conclusions of these gentlemen need not be taken seriously.' His remark applies more widely than he intended.[3]

Miracles and clericalism

The gospels tell of certain 'miracles' performed by Jesus: unexpected healings, dead people brought back to life, multiplications of loaves and fishes. In point of fact the list of miracles attributed to Jesus is by no means long when one compares it with the texts of other religions. Not only is the quantity of them small; the quality of the narratives poses problems that many scholars brush aside too lightly, as we shall see.

Needless to say, the presence of the miraculous in the New Testament has always been the main reason for dismissing these texts as 'legendary'. Renan: 'That the gospels are in large part legendary is obvious, since they are full of miracles and the supernatural.'

We shall see later how gingerly one needs to approach all such declarations made in the name of the 'scientific spirit'. For the present we are merely glancing at what has been said about the miracles, so as to reinforce our wariness as we consider the so-called definitive theories. The scientific spirit that inspires some of these theories denies all possibility of existence to phenomena that do not figure in the list of what science has, to date, succeeded in explaining. Everything else is labelled untruth, or illusion, paranoia, mania.

Here is what has been said by one of the acknowledged masters of gospel criticism, Ernest Havet: 'The first duty imposed by the rationalist principle, which is the basis of all criticism, is that of excluding the supernatural from the life of Jesus. This at once disqualifies the gospel miracles. When criticism refuses to believe the miracle stories, it is under no obligation to adduce proofs in support of its rejection of them: what is recounted is untrue for the simple reason that it could not have happened.'

These 'liberal spirits' were animated – and still are to some degree – by the principle which decrees *a priori* that the gospel texts can contain truth only when they recount 'natural' events, and that they are of necessity manipulated whenever they testify to a fact that science has not yet foreseen.

To decree *a priori* the impossibility of anything at all is hardly compatible with the true scientific spirit. Science makes progress by assimilating experiences that in former times were deemed unthinkable. When a scientist enunciates a system whereby the facts are put through a filter, he ceases to be a scientist and becomes a philosopher.

And what happens when every suggestion of the supernatural is brushed aside with scorn? The miracles recounted in the gospels are explained away in a variety of ways. To the story of the prophet who brought a violent storm to an end by ordering the wind and the waves to be still, Strauss (one of the fathers of rational Christology) has given us a 'simple solution': the disciples and their master had hidden some skins full of oil in their boats; when this oil was poured on the waves the people on the shore thought a miracle had occurred. ...

The evangelists refer to earthquakes at the time of the Passion and Resurrection of Christ. Here is the explanation offered by Robert Ambelain, a freemason, who published a successful book in 1972: the 'earthquakes' felt by the inhabitants of Jerusalem were explosions. The disciples had learned how to use gunpowder from some Chinese experts; they exploded a few charges of it and the people in the city at once thought "Earthquake!" ...

Yet tempers still fray very easily when one advances the hypothesis that many of these works on the origins of Christianity are now hopelessly obsolete, overtaken not only by the progress made by archaeology and exegesis but also by the spirit which inspired them in the first place.

All too often these weighty tomes breathe out an air heavy with clericalism – outwardly the opposite of, but in fact no different from, the clericalism, dogmatism and arrogance with which much of the old-time Christian apologetics blinded us all with science.

This having been said, it should be obvious that for our part we are certainly not going to try to 'prove' the miracles attributed to Jesus by the gospels.

Scornful rejection of them *a priori* and attempts to prove them authentic both seem to us equally pointless. 'We should not let ourselves get bogged down in problems of that sort: what matters is getting at the meaning of these events and their significance for ourselves' (Maggioni).

To tackle the problem of Jesus on the terrain of the 'gospel marvels' is to emulate Bertrand Russell, another master of a certain type of reasoning, who wrote an entire book just to let us know that he 'couldn't be a Christian'. Why? Because although the Christ of the gospels proclaimed a God of love and mercy and even justice, he spoke of the possibility of punishment and thereby introduced the idea of *hell.* Therefore, says our Nobel prize winner, Jesus cannot be God because I do not believe in hell. ...

Anyone who starts from the miracles, or from any particular points in Christ's teaching, in order to explain the gospels ends up in a blind alley; this is true both of Christian apologetics and atheist propaganda. It is akin to taking the bull by the tail instead of the horns. In this case one has to take the bull by the horns by making the effort to sift all possible hypotheses about the origin of Christianity without presuppositions or inflexible programmes of any sort, pseudo-scientific or the reverse.

When one is faced with the problem of the man Jesus – the only man in history to be identified with God, and the man who disrupted history itself – to sidestep the issue (as Russell and so many others have done by running off at tangents or tucking themselves away in cul-de-sacs) is an unacceptable reaction.

It is scientifically, and perhaps also morally, wrong to try to evade the question put by Pilate (*"But who are you?"*)

and take refuge in arguments about hell or the existence of angels or the calming of a storm. These and many other matters are logically subordinate to the main question which was, is and always will be the one put to Jesus by the disciples of John the Baptist: *"Are you the one who is to come or are we to wait for another?"* (Matthew 11).[4]

Daniel Rops: 'What do they matter, these minor puzzles about which so many books get written? The essential enigma is the one posed by this man – a man like us – whose words and actions show his constant mastery of unknown forces: the mystery of a man who belongs in history and yet seems to transcend it.'

The belief hypothesis: history by stages

But what does it mean to be a 'believer'? What goes to make up the *belief hypothesis* today?

Let us remember straightaway that the centuries-old argument over Jesus has been trying to answer one fundamental question: What connection is there between the gospels and history?

We have seen that according to the *'critical' solution* this connection varies from one gospel episode to the next, from one verse to the next, depending on whether one discerns an echo of a real happening or merely an 'addition' on the part of the believing community. In any case the connection is said to be very tenuous; in the view of some critics it is non-existent. The most that can be said about Jesus, according to these scholars, is that he existed and did some preaching, though quite what he preached we do not know. All the same it is perfectly clear (and here these critics are unanimous) that there is no connection whatever between historical fact and the gospels when the latter speak of miracles or point in any way to a supernatural dimension.

The *'mythical' solution* allows of no link whatsoever between genuine history and what the gospels record about Jesus. The mere existence of a man by that name is said to be impossible to assert with any confidence. In any case, whether or not one concedes that he may have existed, he is in no way the originator of any teaching or the exemplar of any life; both the teaching and the life were tacked on to him by some obscure communities that believed in outlandish myths of some kind.

And the *solution of faith*, the belief hypothesis? Here we shall take the present-day position of the oldest and by far the largest numerically of the Christian communities, the Roman Catholic Church.

Apart from any other considerations, the Catholic solution to the problem of the historicity of the gospels can be classed as 'of the centre'. To the 'right' (if such classifications have any meaning) lie the positions of some of the Eastern Orthodox, and to the 'left' the various positions of the Protestants, who not infrequently accept the theories of the critical and mythological schools of thought while at the same time maintaining that such acceptance does not entail abandoning the dimension of faith.

To the question 'What type of historical knowledge is provided by the gospels?' Catholicism insists first and foremost that these four small books 'are not biographies but the Church's own books, and they reflect in part the life of the early Christian community'. They are part history, part preaching. They cannot be thought of as official records or history in the modern sense of the word.

This is the position officially approved by the Pontifical Biblical Commission in 1964 in its *Instruction* dealing explicitly with the historicity of the gospels; this took full account of the results of modern exegesis and accepted many of them.

In the following year the Vatican Council's *Dogmatic Constitution on Divine Revelation* (known as *Dei Verbum*) solemnly reiterated what had been said in the *Instruction.*

With these two documents the Catholic Church put its seal on a principle that by now is generally accepted: the gospels as we now have them were formulated in stages – three at least.

Obviously the *first stage* was Jesus himself, his life and his preaching.

Next – and this is the *second stage* – came the oral preaching of the disciples. The master left them nothing in writing, so the apostles based their proclamation of him on what they themselves remembered and on what was remembered by first-hand witnesses. We shall see later that textual criticism has shown how scrupulously the Church leaders vetted the content of what was preached; this had to obtain the approval of 'those who from the beginning were eyewitnesses and ministers of the Word', as the author of Luke says at the start of that gospel. All the same there is no doubt that the accounts of the life, death, miracles and resurrection of Jesus were drawn up in ways designed to meet preaching needs: thus the message was *summarised* in set formulas, *set out* according to patterns likely to be useful and convenient to the preacher, with *stress laid* on what seemed most important for the type of hearer being addressed at the time. It should not be forgotten that, right from the earliest years, the message was taken to almost all the peoples of the Mediterranean. The prime purpose of the exercise was not to produce a biography of the Messiah but to proclaim a message of salvation, not to train historians but to inspire and educate believers. To quote the 1964 *Instruction:* 'the words and actions of Jesus were interpreted according to the needs of those who were listening'. It was not the 'how' but the 'why' of the Master's life that mattered to the first Christians.

The *third stage* was the editing and production of the written gospels we now have. This took place several decades after the start of oral preaching and apparently arose out of work done on earlier brief collections of 'sayings of Jesus' (which constitute an intermediate stage between the oral preaching and the definitive writings). How did this editing and final production come about, according to the Catholic understanding? The Council document says that the authors of the gospels wrote 'selecting some things from the many which had been handed down by word of mouth or in writing, reducing some of them to a synthesis, explicating some things in view of the situation of their churches, and preserving the form of proclamation – but always in such fashion that they told us the honest truth about Jesus' (*Dei Verbum* 19).

So the evangelists must have done a job not dissimilar to that done by modern newspaper sub-editors on 'copy' sent in by reporters and material provided by news agencies. It is a job of selection, synthesis, presentation and sometimes explanation. The result is the printed newspaper article: something different from the mass of original material but not necessarily any less true to the facts of the matter.

All the same, while stressing that the transition from the Jesus of history to the Jesus of the gospels was not immediate but took place in stages and was the work of the early Christian community, the conciliar document states: 'The Church has firmly and with absolute constancy held, and still holds, that the four gospels, whose historicity she unhesitatingly asserts, faithfully hand on what Jesus the Son of God, during his life among men, really did and taught ...' (*Dei Verbum* 19).

It would serve no useful purpose for us to delve into exactly how the Christian community arrived at the four gospels it considered authentic and discarded about eighty others considered apocryphal. All we need do here is remember that there is a big difference between the first three and the fourth. Matthew, Mark and Luke – though they differ from one another in important respects – are often markedly similar, even in respect of wording.

The line of development in all three is so alike that in

many instances it is possible to lay them out in three columns and read them in parallel at a glance: for this reason they are called the *synoptics* (from the Greek root *sin-op* meaning 'to see together'). Various theories have been suggested to explain this interdependence, among them one that there was a (long since lost) primitive version of Matthew written in Syria after the year 50 which was the basis for Mark, the earliest written gospel we have; Mark also drew on a collection of 'sayings of Jesus'; Luke and the Matthew we have drew in turn on those same texts, via Mark. These are complex problems to which the various specialists – Catholics included – can provide no agreed answers despite much lively discussion.

By contrast the gospel of John does not fit into the series. Certainly it was the latest of the four to be written; but although the writer had access to the other three he followed a completely independent line of development. Side by side with his account of the life and teaching of Jesus, John gives us what might well be called a *fourth stage:* theological reflection; this is almost completely absent from the other three gospels which confine themselves to the bare essentials. Someone has described this text as 'hindsight'. Here the actions and sayings of Jesus are understood, interpreted – and therefore narrated in the light of the mystery of Easter: the passion, death and resurrection of the Christ.

A debt of gratitude

In the next two chapters we shall look at some of the many difficulties that need to be taken into account by both the critical and the mythological schools of thought. We here and now make no secret of the fact that in our opinion reason itself can lead one to conclude – all things considered – that the belief hypothesis is reason's own ultimate resting-place, once it has seen through all the solutions put forward by so-called 'scepticism'.

Within the limits of our own capabilities we shall try to induce that conclusion in our readers, and we shall put forward additional arguments over and above those already adduced. As always we shall try to remain on the solid ground of what is beyond dispute – at least in the light of what recent research has made available – and shun the little tricks practised by dogmatists of every hue.

After so much philosophical colouring of history, perhaps the time has come for an honest and courageous attempt to *distinguish what is known from what is believed.*

If such an undertaking is less impossible today than in the past, believers owe this to the labours of the scholars – even those scholars whose conclusions faith cannot accept. This debt of gratitude to the so-called 'sceptics' is unfortunately not always honoured by Christians.

In the next chapter we shall be examining the critical hypothesis in particular, and in the following one we shall go into a few questions that directly challenge the mythical hypothesis.

But this dividing line is far from inflexible, for more reasons than one. In the first place, our aim is to draw attention to a few points that provide food for thought and leave room for further development. In the second place, both of the negative hypotheses can often be found in works by one and the same author, although the mixtures vary from author to author.

Let one illustrious example suffice: Alfred Loisy. In the introduction to his '*Origins of Christianity*' he writes that he is 'obliged in all humility to admit to having not yet discovered that Jesus never existed'. After this ironic thrust at what he calls the 'clamorous conjecturings of the mythologists', he nonetheless makes a few concessions to his opponents in that party. He in fact acknowledges that 'the role of myth in the Christian tradition is as undeniable as it was inevitable'; and that 'if Jesus and the myth together bring Christianity, the messianic myth brought Jesus.'

Going even further than that, in another work he attempted a kind of synthesis of the two positions, though still giving pride of place to that of the textual critics: 'Neither Jesus without myth, nor myth without Jesus.'

So although our next chapter is principally concerned with the 'critics' it will not overlook the 'mythologists'. Often they are one and the same.

Notes

1 One explanation of it has been offered by Luis Alonso-Schökel, a present-day biblical specialist: 'The devotees of textual criticism had been living in an ivory tower, imprisoned in the biblical text. They had been drawn into that sort of prison by their own philosophical and religious concepts, one of which was fundamental denial that the Bible has any supernatural value. This led to their developing a root and branch mistrust of the historicity of the facts narrated by the biblical authors. Then the army of archaeologists broke down the barriers erected by the bookmen and theorists, and went in search of facts and independent data. ... The learned men at their book-strewn desks set about consolidating their own positions, treating with lofty disdain the results obtained by the no less learned men armed with picks and shovels. And the archaeologists went on digging away, undermining quite a number of the textual critics' constructions. ... Some of the critics tried to have it both ways: they would recognise the archaeologists' results but declare them to be in agreement with their own theories; or they would admit that incontrovertible data are worth more than well-constructed hypotheses and then add that the facts were conspicuous proof of the rightness of the hypotheses. ...'

2 Let us repeat that we have every respect and admiration for the labours of the textual critics and form-critics of the last couple of centuries; we are familiar with their methods and we admire their erudition and ingenuity. Nonetheless we cannot help feeling suspicious of the excessive assurance shown by all too many of them, all fully convinced that they have found the one and only answer to the enigma of the New Testament. The history of much radical criticism is a history of many successes and cultural advances, but it is also one of frequent gaffes and strategic withdrawals. Or, what is worse, of stubborn defence of untenable positions. It is also one of mutual scorn and derision among the critics themselves, of constant overtakings of one 'definitive' solution after another. There would seem to be room for an injection of humility after all the defeats the various schools of thought have inflicted on one another.

3 Some psychologists' studies of Jesus's character provide an excellent example of the inconsistency of the rationalists. Eminent professors, although avowed partisans of the non-historicity of the gospels, have nevertheless seized on minor details in the gospel narratives to prove that Jesus was many different kinds of maniac and suffered from a wide variety of phobias. In their boundless faith in the reliability of these particular gospel details they far surpass in credulity the most simple and devout of Christian believers.

4 Pascal: 'How distasteful I find all this quibbling over the eucharistic elements, etc. If the Gospel is true, where is the difficulty over all these other things?' And Novalis, the German poet: 'If God was able to become man, surely he can become bread and wine too.'

7.

Criticism's crosses

When one is dealing with facts, history, real life and eye-witness accounts, any postulates unwarrantably described as 'scientific' are worth no more than theological ones. Both varieties have to be thrust aside. Not because they are scientific or theological in nature but simply because they are postulates – that is to say a priori convictions. One cannot be too much on one's guard against the dishonest misuse of the word 'science' and its derivatives that has been all too evident since the 18th century. There isn't a single obscurantism, fanaticism, trickery or downright stupidity (from corn-cures to racism) that hasn't at one time or another claimed the backing of 'science'.

R. L. BRUCKBERGER

I THE MOST UNLIKELY OF MESSIAHS

How is it that he alone, of all the many aspiring messiahs, achieved success?

'This prophet, who at the most aroused curiosity tinged with sympathy among the ordinary people of Galilee, was one of those claimants to the title of Messiah ... who from time to time emerged in Israel. His failure was total. Therefore he was mistaken in his claim. All likelihood and all logic demanded that his name and his work should be completely forgotten, as was the case with so many others in Israel who believed themselves to be somebody special.'

That is how Charles Guignebert, one of the most eminent modern representatives of the critical school and who for thirty years occupied the chair of History of Christianity at the Sorbonne, summed up the life and fate of Jesus.

Guignebert began his last (posthumous) work by admitting that 'the original cause of the emergence of Christianity was the initiative of Jesus the Nazarene, who lived in Palestine at the time of Augustus and Tiberius. The texts do not tell us much about him but they do at least inform us that he was a real man and not in any way a compound of myth and symbol.'

He thus shut the door on the mythical school. And yet it was not believers but the doubly sceptical mythologists who showed that Guignebert and his fellow critics were entering a blind alley. As we shall see.

According to Guignebert, 'all likelihood and all logic demanded that the name and work of Jesus should be completely forgotten, as was the case with so many others in Israel who believed themselves to be somebody special'. Why then was Jesus the only one of them to achieve 'dazzling success' (in Guignebert's own phrase)?

The critical school admits that to turn the obscure Jesus into the Messiah of a world-wide faith was a task of considerable difficulty (and that the difficulties would have been far fewer in the case of any of the other claimants to the messianic throne).

To effect such a transformation (unthinkable for many good reasons, as we shall see) the disciples had to get the better of a number of disappointments: that ignominious death, all the frustrated hopes of a return in glory that did not materialise; above all they had to accept, themselves, a new concept of the Messiah – a concept not only new but downright shocking.

Everything would have been far more logical if that faith – if it was to arise at all – had centred on one of the other claimants; those others were far more in line with what was expected of the Messiah in first-century Palestine. Yet he alone, in the four thousand years of Jewish history, has won the day.

He alone, of all the many religious leaders who have aspired to spiritual conquest of the western world (using methods very different from his), has truly conquered it – apparently definitively.

Pontius Pilate, who was able to condemn Jesus to death without in any way prejudicing his own career, lost his job – and some say his head – for having dared to maltreat the followers of another messiah. That particular claimant to the title had set the whole region of Samaria in ferment by promising his disciples that on Mount Garizim, sacred to the Samaritans, he would 'show' them some of Moses's garments. Instead of the mystical 'showing' his followers were treated to the Roman cavalry, sent by Pilate to disperse them. The Samaritans lodged a protest with Pilate's superior, Vitellius, Roman legate in Syria with full powers over the eastern province. Vitellius, after consulting the emperor, stripped Pilate of his command and sent him back to Rome to be tried.

The case of Jesus had caused Pilate no trouble at all. Those few uncouth Galileans who took Jesus seriously certainly had no great following or influential friends to create any rumpus. Yet quite illogically history has failed to record even the name of the powerful Christ of Samaria, whose followers succeeded in wrecking the career of the most powerful Roman in Palestine. Why did the messianic hope not become concentrated around that 'church', which obviously was far better equipped to win for itself a future? Why did history sweep away the faith of the Samaritans, whereas that of the Galileans has transformed the world?

Where Jesus is concerned the historical constants do not apply. Those laws which are said to govern human affairs prove ineffective: the weak inexplicably triumph and the strong fade away. According to the celebrated Couchoud, who later denied that Jesus ever existed: 'There are no analogies for his case; according to all the laws of history known to us, the emergence of Christianity is an incredible absurdity and the most bizarre of all miracles.'

There are a few indications that even Barabbas, the one whom Pilate suggested might be exchanged for Jesus, was an aspiring messiah. According to Matthew, Barabbas was 'a notorious prisoner'; Mark adds that 'along with other seditious persons he had caused a revolt' and Luke specifies that 'the revolt occurred in the city' – that is to say in Jerusalem, where all who claimed messiahship habitually made their way.

Perhaps there was even a community, a 'church' of Barabbites or Barabbans. If there was, we know of its founder only because he happens to come in at the end of the gospel narratives. Therein the principal character goes to his death and then triumphs over all. The minor character is set free (perhaps to resume his messianic propaganda) but disappears for ever.

Towards the end of his life Loisy summarised the little that, in his view, any historian can say for certain about Jesus:

'He was an itinerant preacher, a prophet with a single message. His teachings, if any, were not collected and recorded. In a gesture of religious enlightenment he chose to take his message about the Kingdom to Jerusalem. His presence in the city caused an uproar. He was arrested and summarily tried by the Roman authorities in circumstances unknown to us.'

That is the type of thinking that caused the mythologists to assert that even the vestigial historicity acknowledged by Loisy and his colleagues in the critical school had to be denied. They objected, quite rightly, that the more one 'reduces' Jesus the more one increases the mystery. The more insignificant one makes him, the less one can understand the already incomprehensible process whereby in no time at all (as we shall see) he became the Christ, on a par with Yahweh.

According to the critical school there is no difference, historically speaking, between the Nazarene and the Samaritan messiah, or between him and Barabbas. Or even between Jesus and Theudas, a 'prophet' who around the year AD 44 drew the people to Jerusalem in another outburst of fanaticism. The waters of the Jordan, he promised, would divide and allow him to pass. ... Like the Samaritans before them, the followers of Theudas were met by the Roman cavalry, sent by the new procurator of Palestine Cuspius Fadus. After much skirmishing Theudas's disorderly mob was dispersed and his own head was taken to Jerusalem to figure in a Roman triumph. So the prophet of the Jordan met a glorious death in battle – an end far more likely to stimulate the faith of his followers than a shameful execution on a cross. Yet we know nothing about the church of Theudas, if there ever was one.

And what about that Egyptian Jew who a few years later, about AD 58, led the usual crowd to the Mount of Olives proclaiming that at the sound of his voice the walls of Jerusalem would fall to the ground and the people would be able to advance towards the inauguration of the longed-for messianic era? The then procurator, Felix, rode out at the head of the usual cavalry. It was a bloody encounter: the crowd was fanatical and more than 400 got killed. But – and this is worthy of note – once the battle was over no trace of the leader was to be found. The Egyptian Jew disappeared; some even said they had seen him passing unhurt through the Roman forces, as if under God's protection. What a superb opportunity for the birth of the myth of the One sent by Yahweh, for attributing divinity to so prestigious a candidate for the messiahship! But if the Egyptian Jew of the Mount of Olives had any disciples we do not know what they were called: for history hasn't recorded so much as the name of that particular messiah.

Finally here is Bar Kokeba: he was the ultimate in Jewish messianism, not only chronologically but ideally as well. His name was Simeon; the other name was given him in acknowledgment of his messianic entitlements. In Aramaic Bar Kokeba means 'son of the star', a term applied only to the Messiah. Moreover the best-known of the rabbis and doctors of the Law, Akiba the Great, publicly recognised him as the Christ. Even though 'all the times had come and gone', even though many Jews considered the days of expectation to have become the days of disappointment, the impressiveness of Simeon the Magnificent and the official recognition accorded to him by the priests eventually resulted in his drawing everyone along with him. In AD 132 Bar Kokeba succeeded in driving the Romans out of Jerusalem. Enthusiasm knew no bounds: new coins were struck bearing the inscription 'First Year of Israel's Redemption', i.e. the first year of the messianic era.

Further exciting victories followed. But when Rome counter-attacked the struggle reached terrible proportions. According to the historian Dion Cassius, the resistance of the Jews – convinced that they were fighting under the banner of Israel's Christ – was so fanatical that the Roman legionaries had to destroy with much bloodshed a good fifty fortresses and nearly a thousand towns and villages.

When their astounding resistance – 'which amazed the whole world' according to Dion Cassius – ended in the second total destruction of Israel, their faith in Bar Kokeba crumbled. The priests who had called him 'son of the star' changed the name to Bar Koseba – 'son of untruth'. Belief in Simeon, the officially accredited Messiah, died out completely after his glorious defeat in battle. Yet belief in Jesus, the officially discredited Messiah, survived his inglorious defeat – the shameful death meted out to slaves.

Leaving aside the fate of the other candidates for messiahship, the plain fact is that the development which took place in the wake of Jesus lacked all raison d'être. The belief in him that arose in Jewish circles, and grew into the conviction that he was more than just a man, is an absolutely unique phenomenon that defies explanation. An authentic 'miracle' both culturally and historically. Paul of Tarsus was right when he said that faith in that crucified Christ was '*an outrage for the Jews and folly for the pagans*'.

The much derided conclusion reached by believers, who assign mystery a part in the growth of Christianity, is less irrational – to those who are familiar with the problem – than the absurdities (described as 'scientific') concocted by the critical school of thought. It is not believers who say this but scholars of the mythological persuasion, who have taken issue with the critical school because they recognise that the transition from the Jesus of history to the Christ of faith was a logical impossibility for the world of Judaism.[1]

II AN IMPOSSIBILITY AMONG JEWS

A Jew divinised by Jews: the most absurd of all hypotheses

'Anyone trying to explain Christian origins has to make a fundamental choice.

'Jesus is one problem.

'Christianity is another.

'You cannot solve the one without making the other insoluble.

'If you tackle the problem of Jesus, you have to go the way of Renan, Loisy, Guignebert. You will describe more or less colourfully a messianic agitator, a teacher at the time of the last of the Herods. You will give him characteristics that enable you to fit him into history. If you are a clever critic the portrait you paint will be plausible, and you will doubtless merit some applause.

'But then Christianity will present itself as an insoluble problem.

'For how could that obscure, insignificant teacher have been transmuted into the Son of God, the inexhaustible subject of Christian worship and theology?

'Here we are right off the beaten track of history. There is not a single analogy. Christianity is an unbelievable absurdity and the most bizarre of miracles.'

Those stringent comments were written by Couchoud, the mythologist. They infuriated Loisy. For Loisy had indeed painted a plausible picture and merited some applause; but then he was indeed unable to explain the rise of Christianity.

In point of fact Couchoud and his fellow-mythologists eventually prevailed over most of the scholars, with the result that by now very few experts accept in full the theories of the critics who until a few decades ago were acclaimed as the unconquerable masters of the scientific method.

To suppose that in Jewish circles any man could have been mistaken for Yahweh and therefore worshipped, and this not after many generations but within only a few years of his degrading death, means 'having no genuine knowledge of Jews – or else forgetting it all'.

It also means, as St Augustine pointed out, admitting the possibility of 'the greatest of all miracles'. In other words it means admitting that a faith like this one was able to take root in such circles without some 'miracle' to germinate it.

Here is Couchoud again:

'In many areas of the empire it could be a fairly simple matter to deify one created being or another. But among one people at least, the Jews, it was totally out of the question. They worshipped Yahweh, the one and only God, the transcendent God whose name was never spoken, whose portrait was never drawn, who was separated by an unbridgeable gulf from every created being. To equate any man with Yahweh was the utmost sacrilege, the ultimate abomination.

'The Jews honoured the emperor, but they were ready to let themselves be stoned rather than whisper an admission that the emperor was a god. They would equally have let themselves be stoned rather than say the same of Moses.

'Would it have come at all naturally to Paul, a Jew of Jewish parentage, to equate a man with Yahweh? This is the miracle that I myself refuse to believe. …

'How can one possibly maintain that Paul, a Jew from Cilicia educated as a Pharisee, would have had no compunction whatever about applying to a Jew of his own day from Galilee the sacred texts that speak of Yahweh?'

To argue along the line Couchoud here attacks – and the critics did so argue for a long time – one would indeed have to lack all genuine knowledge of Jews – or else forget it all.

One would have to forget …

One would have to forget that the Jews underwent collective martyrdom and the destruction of their country rather than accept not the divinisation of the Roman emperor but simply the portraits of the emperor-god painted on the standards borne by the Roman legionaries in Jerusalem.

One would have to forget that throughout the four thousand years of Jewish religious history there is no other trace of the inexplicable divinisation process that was applied to Jesus. Not only that: not one of the disciples of the many pseudo-messiahs ever thought of putting his own Christ on a par with Yahweh. So Jesus is not merely the only one to survive the defeat inflicted by death; he is also the only one whom any of his disciples have dared to identify with God. Jesus is the only Jew ever worshipped by any Jews.

One would have to forget that the very idea of worshipping a man scandalises Semites today no less than it did when Jesus did not deny that he was the 'Son of God': '*Then the high priest rent his garments and cried out: "He has blasphemed! What need have we of witnesses now? There! You have heard the blasphemy. What is your opinion?" They answered: "He deserves death!"* ' (Matthew 26). It has been remarked that Mohammed and Islam represent a revolt by the Semitic race against the outrageous Christian claim that a mere man was God's equal. On the cupola of the mosque of Omar in Jerusalem there is an inscription calling on Christians to give up claiming the impossible, to abandon their illusion: 'Jesus is simply the son of Mary, a man among men.'

One would have to forget that worship of Jesus meant that a group of Jews had gone even further than the pagans, whom they viewed with horror precisely because of their propensity to invent myths and deify human beings. One god more or one god less in the Roman pantheon occasioned no surprise: after all, there was a shrine even for 'the unknown god' – just in case one of them had got forgotten. ... Yet the Jews who raised an obscure preacher to the level of Yahweh are supposed, according to the critical school, to have imagined something that even the most fanatical adorer of the emperor never suggested: that this Jesus was God 'even before his birth'. Anyone rash enough to say that of a Caesar would have been laughed to scorn by the Romans themselves. The pagan philosopher Celsus strongly objected – in the name of reason and of classical culture's common-sense – to the outlandish Christian cult which surpassed in extravagance anything that the later years of the Roman empire produced: 'The body of a god cannot be like your body; it cannot eat like yours or speak like yours. Is the blood in your veins anything like what courses through the veins of a god?'

One would have to forget that, even granted the inadmissible (i.e. that the idea of an historical incarnation of Yahweh did arise in the Jewish mind), never would that idea have taken the extreme form of 'incarnation by way of the womb of a mere woman'.

All that and much besides[2] was overlooked by the critics, those masters of the rational method and experts in matters concerning the Israel of old. They were duly ridiculed by the mythological school, which attacked them on their own ground of science and scepticism.

Who is of 'sound intellect'?

In 1934 the philosopher Piero Martinetti, one of the later generation of critics, wrote that the theory that Christianity arose out of the hallucinations of some of Jesus's disciples (who thought they had seen him risen from the dead) 'is the only theory that anyone of sound intellect can accept'.

Yet it was scholars as rationalist as himself, not believers, who demonstrated that the theory that pious Jews bowed the knee to some mystic, some down-at-heel prophet, declaring him to be God, is *not a theory that anyone of sound intellect can accept.*

More recently Rudolf Augstein, founder and editor of the well-known German weekly *Der Spiegel*, set some of his best reporters to work on an 'inquiry' into Jesus. Several years' work led to the conclusion that the gospels have no reliable historical basis whatever. Jesus is a 'son of man', and the churches may as well shut up shop. Augstein and his men trot out all the theories already advanced time and again by the various members of the critical school; but the objections of the mythologists also find an echo in the editor's own contribution: 'In practice one has to exclude the possibility that in Galilee or in Judaea any Jew could have been held to be – or declare himself to be – the Son of God. He would have been a madman to do so.'

However, Augstein thinks he can dispose of the problem by a shift of responsibility: Jesus did not declare himself on a par with Yahweh, nor could he possibly have done so; the assertions to that effect in the gospels were therefore added by his disciples.

But the disciples too were Jews. Why should their master stop short of such folly and his disciples, members of his own race, run headlong into it?

To do so they would not only have had to overcome their own convictions and go dead against all inherited tradition; they would also have had to defy the powerful institutions of official legalistic Judaism, ready to ensnare anyone who cast doubt on the oneness, transcendence and total otherness of God.

Those implacable confessional traps closed on Jesus and sent him to his cross. They snapped again, according to the Acts of the Apostles, to catch the first disciple who dared to proclaim in public the equation of God with a certain man. Stephen, venerated by the Church as the first of her martyrs, '*filled with the Holy Spirit, gazed into heaven and saw the glory of God, and said: "Behold, I see the heavens opened and the Son of Man standing at the right hand of God." Then they cried out with a loud voice and stopped their ears and rushed at him, all together; and having driven him out of the city they stoned him*' (Acts 7).

Their reaction was typical of the root and branch rejection suffered throughout history by other Jewish converts to Christianity.

It was only thanks to a much-publicised but quite unreliable distortion of the evidence that the critical school was able to claim that Jesus's disciples effected the divinisation process quite naturally, simply on the basis of a few rumours circulating after their master's burial, some hysterical hallucinations on the part of a few women, and the removal of his body by a gardener. Or (even worse) that the disciples themselves concealed the body and then declared to all and sundry that the man who was crucified had risen from the dead.

A bridge between Jesus and the Christ

But there is more to be said, and it is Guignebert the critic who says it:

'The pitiful and scandalous crucifixion had thrown the disciples into the deepest grief and despair.'

Yet men in that state of mind pulled themselves together and decided – unlike the followers of all the other messiahs who never got over the defeat of their leaders – to defy not only the Jewish and Roman authorities, not only the threat of death, but also the voice of their own conscience, which must have reminded them that Scripture pronounced terrible curses on heretics, apostates, blasphemers – on themselves, in fact.

But there is more still, Guignebert insists. The faith of these incredible men must have had to contend with another 'painful defeat': their Christ's return in glory, which they expected within a very short time, failed to materialise. 'The great miracle did not occur, but the disciples' faith survived this second disappointment too.'

The Czech Marxist Machovec, atheist author of a book on Jesus for atheists, asks:

'How were the followers of Jesus, Peter's group in particular, ever able to overcome the terrible disappointment, the scandal of the cross, and turn it to good account in a successful campaign? How was a prophet whose predictions came to nought ever able to become the inspiration for the greatest of the world's religions? Generation after generation of historians have asked themselves these questions and they are still asking them to this day. ...'

Bridging the gap between the death of Jesus and the birth of Christianity is a far more difficult undertaking than the critics are willing to admit. In fact they all stop short when the time comes for building a bridge between the obscure Jesus of history and the brilliant Christ of faith.

Looking for props and stays

The fact is that miracle was accorded full right of entry into the 'reconstructions' made by these experts who were so determined to exclude the miraculous altogether.

Even Loisy began to falter towards the end of his life – a life devoted to weighing and re-weighing the verses of the New Testament and denying the authenticity of one of them after another. In 1933, in the introduction to his last work on the origins of Christianity, he wrote: 'Any account of the beginnings of this faith resembles, willy nilly, a shakily built construction.'

The mythologists' attacks on him had succeeded in leaving him puzzled as to how the Jesus of history had become the Christ of faith. Of the events that followed the crucifixion he wrote: 'The historian can give only probable answers, based on a few scraps of evidence.'

He had realised how impossible it is to explain how a few years after the death of one Jew, another Jew called Paul could write what he did write in the second chapter of his letter to the Philippians:

'*Therefore God has highly exalted him and bestowed on him the name that is above every name, so that at the name of Jesus every knee should bow, in heaven and on earth and under the earth, and every tongue confess that Jesus Christ is the Lord, to the glory of God the Father.*'

So, faced with the mockery of the mythologists – and himself increasingly conscious that the theory of a Jew divinised by other Jews was becoming less and less tenable – Loisy made one final desperate throw. In an attempt to prop up his tottering edifice he set about denying the authenticity of Paul's witness to his worship of Jesus. Banishing all thoughts of what he had previously asserted, he declared that the Pauline texts which failed to fit his divinisation theory were later additions, interpolations.

But interpolated by whom? 'By a mysterious mystical sect that flourished at the end of the first century', replied Loisy.

At that point, however, even his most faithful disciples rebelled.

In Italy there was a loud protest from Buonaiuti – himself already excommunicated for having propagated Loisy's ideas: 'If now the historical Paul, the Paul of the Letters, vanishes into thin air to get lost in the clouds of second-century gnostic speculation, gospel criticism (already being confined within stricter and stricter limits by manuscript evidence) will have to be undertaken all over again: and were that to be the case, it would have to be undertaken in closer conformity with orthodox tradition.' That is to say, in closer conformity with the belief hypothesis. With some bitterness, given his own sufferings in the cause of Loisy's theories, Buonaiuti concluded: 'A pretty pass to come to, after so many excommunications!'

Someone else then attempted to salvage the absurd hypothesis of the divinised Jew by presenting a highly coloured reproduction of the portrait of the 'obscure preacher' in whom the faith originated.

'The abyss between man and God was bridged because Jesus was a man with the gifts of a medium, a faith-healer. He was a successful practitioner of para-psychology whose powers, impressive although in no way supernatural, produced a "shock reaction" violent enough to give rise to the beliefs of his disciples.'

It's an ingenious theory, but no serious scholar has ever in fact accepted it.

In the Jewish world there had always been a quiet conviction that God could imbue men with some faint traces of his own power. There are stories not only about biblical prophets but also about simple rabbis who healed incurables, made the dead speak, held back the waters of rivers and seas.

Elijah, Elisha and Moses all (according to scripture) performed 'wonders'. Yet not a single Jew was tempted to regard any of those 'wonder-workers' as of divine origin. The true wonder-worker was always Yahweh, and only Yahweh. God had quite simply deigned to give expression to his omnipotence through a human channel.

Moreover, the wonders worked by Jesus's disciples are narrated without any fuss.

In the Acts of the Apostles, chapter 5:

'*Many miracles and wonders were worked among the people of Jerusalem by the hands of the apostles,*' so much so that '*they carried the sick out into the streets and laid them on beds and pallets, so that when Peter passed by his shadow at least might fall on some of them. The people also came from the towns round about, bringing the sick and those afflicted by evil spirits, and all were healed.*'

Exactly the same sorts of cure, when effected by Jesus himself, are said by some critics to have triggered the divinisation process.

Why, then, was that process not triggered in Peter's case, or in the case of the deacon, Philip, who brought '*great happiness*' to Samaria by healing large numbers of people?

Why were these two 'wonder-workers' acclaimed simply as '*men of God*' (the traditional Judaic expression) and not as '*sons of God*'?

A great deal more than the cure of a man possessed, or even the resuscitation of a man deceased, was required in Israel – then or at any time – before any mortal man could be equated with Yahweh.[3]

The spark and the explosion

Those are some of the reasons why Couchoud (himself convinced that Jesus's divinity had to be denied 'scientifically' and not with the aid of childish hypotheses) asserted that if the rise of Christianity is to be explained, 'this man has to be struck off the list of historical personages'.

If it is impossible to entertain the supposition that a Jew of flesh and blood was divinised by his contemporaries, then one is bound to think that it all began with a myth. An idea, not a person: 'the idea of a divine being who redeems the human race by an expiatory sacrifice and is shortly to reappear to pass judgment on humanity.'

Loisy retorted irritably that if his own hypothesis led into a blind alley, the one advanced by the mythologists was no less of a dead end: 'We have better things to do than refute those who think that behind what is narrated about Jesus there is no real man but only a myth. If these mythologists were to become too insistent we should simply ask them: where is the match?'

In other words, where is the spark that set light to the great Christian fire if in the first place there was no real person, no 'founder', no 'fire-raiser'? Even Roger Garaudy, the Marxist philosopher, has recently said of Christianity: 'If a brazier was set alight, that is enough to prove that there must have been some flame to set light to it.'

But the mythologists' reply is no less simple: 'Where is the atomic explosion needed in order to dispose of the heap of reasons why the divinisation of a man was an impossibility among Jews? You critics are blowing out your own match when you leave Jesus with only a vestigial historical existence; much more than the sort of flame you envisage was needed to set off that conflagration, to allow of that historical absurdity that you take for granted. On your hypothesis, the gigantic effect (Christianity) bears no relation whatever to the cause (Jesus) – whom you try to outdo when you make him more and more evanescent. The principle of causality has some validity in the sphere of history as well as in that of physics; but you ignore it.'

While the mythologists think in terms of a solar system without any sun at its centre, the critics suggest one centred on a small, pallid, evanescent moon.

Be that as it may, the credit for having proved that the divinisation of Jesus was not a lengthy process demanding much time goes to the 'sceptics', both critics and mythologists, and not to believers. Between them they have proved that for the very first generation of Christians his divine nature was already an established fact.

And in so doing they have at once increased the difficulties that the 'negative' hypotheses have to contend with – as we shall soon see.

He was straightaway regarded as on a par with Yahweh

From the earliest days of scientific study of the New Testament the critics have always made great efforts to determine which parts of the gospel accounts can be considered the most ancient – the assumption being that the earlier an incident or a piece of teaching was recorded, the greater the chances are that those particular verses are authentic.

It is now generally agreed that Mark's gospel, which is considered to reflect what was preached by Peter, was the earliest of the four to be composed, and may well have existed in writing before the destruction of Jerusalem in AD 70. Within this already 'early' text scholars have distinguished even earlier 'strata', i.e. accounts of certain episodes taken direct from the very earliest oral preaching about Jesus. Three of these are worth examining.

1. In the second chapter of Mark: Jesus was preaching at Capernaum, and '*they came, bringing to him a paralytic carried by four men. And when they could not get near him because of the crowd, they removed the roof above him; and when they had made an opening they lowered the stretcher on which the paralytic lay. And when Jesus saw their faith he said to the paralytic: "My son, your sins are forgiven*

you." Some scribes who were present thought to themselves: "How can this man talk like that? He is blaspheming. Who can forgive sins except God?" Jesus, sensing what they were thinking, said to them: "Why do you have these thoughts in your hearts? ... To prove to you that the Son of man has authority on earth to forgive sins" – he said to the paralytic – "I order you: get up, pick up your stretcher and go home." And the man got up, picked up his stretcher at once and walked out in sight of them all; they were all astounded and praised God saying "We have never seen anything like this".'

2. Also in the second chapter: Some Pharisees became angry on seeing Jesus's disciples plucking ears of grain in a cornfield on the sabbath – when work of all kinds was forbidden. Jesus told the protesting Pharisees: "*The Son of man is master even of the sabbath.*"

3. In the third chapter: Again on the sabbath; a man with a withered hand entered the synagogue, and the Pharisees watched Jesus '*to see whether he would heal him on the sabbath, so that they might bring an accusation against him*'. Jesus cured the sick man. '*The Pharisees went out and immediately began to plot with the Herodians against him, discussing how to destroy him.*'

These three episodes reflect some of the very earliest teaching about Jesus. So the process of putting a man on a par with God was already complete by the time this earliest preaching got under way. Within at most a single generation after his death, a group of Jews was attributing to the man Jesus the authority that belonged to God alone: the authority to forgive sins and the authority to set aside the sabbath laws. And the author of Mark, who was certainly a Palestinian Jew, recounts without the slightest embarrassment these outrageous stories about a God-man. Nor does he conceal the fact that in Jewish eyes such actions could not be allowed to go unpunished. In the face of violation of the sabbath – even on humanitarian grounds – and confronted with the impiety of a man who claimed an authority that was the prerogative of Yahweh alone, Jewish sects which regarded one another with extreme suspicion came together and made common cause.

Thus in these three very old accounts found in Mark we have further confirmation that, culturally speaking, it was impossible in that milieu for a mere man to be divinised. But we also have confirmation that divinisation of Jesus did occur, and that it occurred straightaway. It was not arrived at only after several generations; it was proclaimed by Jews contemporary with the obscure preacher himself. The gulf between Yahweh and mortal man was bridged immediately.

So the critical school, by burrowing about and identifying the earliest strands of Christian preaching, has made its own theory about the origins of Christianity less tenable, rationally, than ever.

But it has done even more to tarnish its own 'scientific' image by discovering the *kerygma* – a discovery that has also greatly discomfited the mythologists. Both schools of thought now lose even more of their credibility.

III THE KERYGMA'S ANSWER

The kerygma's surprises: the faith was entire from the start

Kerygma is a Greek word meaning 'a spoken proclamation made by a herald'. For some time now the term has been used by scholars to describe the first brief proclamation of 'the good news' by the 'apostolic heralds', the earliest preachers. A call to conversion and salvation addressed to the crowds. A short formula, not unlike a slogan, that sums up in a few words the 'life, death, resurrection and return in glory' of Jesus the Nazarene. Kerygmatic formulas can be detected within a New Testament text because their language and style differ from those of the main body of the text.

These primitive preaching formulas were repeated word for word in the letters of Paul and also in the Acts of the Apostles; we now have them in the form in which those authors first met them. So the discovery of the kerygma, an outstanding achievement on the part of the scholars, has allowed us to recover – miraculously intact – the oral tradition about Jesus that preceded the written Gospel.

Examples of the kerygma are to be found in what is generally thought to be the earliest written Christian document, Paul's letter to the Thessalonians composed not later than AD 52. The fragments of settled oral tradition and Christian liturgy which Paul incorporated in that letter have been dated very close to the year – between AD 30 and 36 – of Jesus's death; to within five or ten years, that is, of the Nazarene's disappearance.

The outstanding importance of the discovery of the kerygma lies in the fact that we are now able to establish scientifically that within a very few years of Jesus's disappearance all the fundamental content of Christianity was already present just as we know it today. In the kerygma the historical facts about the man Jesus and the meaning of his death and resurrection in the context of salvation were already inseparably linked.

Here, within perhaps ten years of his death, is witness to the Jesus of history; but here too is witness to the fact that he had then already become the Christ of faith.

So both the critical school and the mythological school, who themselves detected the kerygmatic formulas, have effectively faced themselves with greater difficulties than ever.

The critical school has to reckon with new, decisive proof that the divinisation of Jesus occurred straightaway. And it occurred in a Jewish milieu. Not in a Hellenistic milieu, as was suggested by those who tried to by-pass the difficulty by asserting that the faith arose in some unspecified place in the eastern Mediterranean.

The mythologists find themselves deprived of the mainstay of their argument – time-lag. For them, Jesus is a god who was *slowly* humanised in the course of several generations. But the kerygma has demonstrated that if Christianity did grow out of some myth, that myth was *immediately* anchored to the historical reality of Jesus the Nazarene, about whom the very earliest preaching at once provided biographical details.

The Christ of faith has his roots in the Jesus of history: this is the unequivocal meaning of the kerygma.

The kerygmatic fragment in the first letter to the Corinthians

For a clearer understanding, let us examine a well-known and undisputed example of kerygma in chapter 15 of Paul's first letter to the Corinthians, which was written not later than AD 57.

Paul introduces this fragment from the earlier tradition by saying explicitly: *'I passed on to you in the first place what I had been taught myself.'* Then come the formulas taken straight from the oral tradition: *'that Christ died for our sins, in accordance with the scriptures; that he was buried; that on the third day he was raised to life, in accordance with the scriptures; that he appeared first to Cephas and then to the twelve. Next he appeared to more than five hundred of the brethren at the same time, most of whom are still alive although some have died. Then he appeared to James, then to all the apostles. ...'*

Here we have a résumé of the faith as it was presented not so very long after the death of Jesus. The proclamation here recorded by Paul perhaps dates from the year 40. If it does – and it is the critics who say that it does – we know how the Christian faith was preached from the beginning.

And we discover that from the start the historical facts about Jesus were intertwined with the theological message of salvation: '*Christ died*' (historical datum); '*for our sins, in accordance with the scriptures*' (datum of faith); '*he was buried*' (historical datum); '*on the third day he was raised to life, in accordance with the scriptures*' (historical datum and datum of faith combined). Then more historical detail: Cephas, the twelve, the 500 brethren, James, the apostles.

Before introducing this kerygmatic fragment Paul explains its value in the context of salvation: '*Now, brethren, I would remind you of the Gospel I preached to you, which you received, in which you stand firm, and through which you are saved if you hold it fast.*' Only God can effect salvation; yet this strict ex-Pharisee states as a matter of course that faith in Jesus can do so too.

If any proof were needed that the process of divinisation took place immediately (and inexplicably from a purely historical point of view) that proof is provided by the kerygma. Not only by that one fragment but by the many others of the same type, here and there throughout the New Testament, which raise serious difficulties for critics and mythologists alike – but especially for the latter.

All the other heroes of myth are set against the vaguest of backgrounds, in a pre-history lacking all geographical location. In the case of Jesus, even the kerygma provides chronological detail, and lists specific events that were open to contemporary verification (many of the 500 brethren 'are still alive'). This is current reporting, not myth creation.

Faced with the kerygma how can one possibly maintain that Christianity began with a myth that little by little took shape and substance around the obscure, perhaps only legendary, figure of Jesus? How can one possibly maintain, in view of what is now known of the earliest Christian preaching dating from around the year 40, that Jesus was invented in Rome after the year 100 so as to justify belief in a myth?

Some more supporting evidence

In 1935, not long after Couchoud had popularised his mythological theory, news came of a papyrus (known as P 52 or the Greek Rylands) that had been found by archaeologists working in Egypt. It was a mere fragment containing only 114 Greek characters, but it was part of the gospel of John. And those characters had been written down not later than the year 125. Now, nobody disputes that John's gospel was the latest of the four. But the mythologists, and some of the critics too, based their theories on the assumption that it did not exist until fairly late in the second century – for only a comparable lapse of time would allow of full development of the Jesus myth. It has since been proved that the fragment found in Egypt was copied from an original written in Ephesus around the year 100. Yet according to the mythologists Jesus was not even 'invented' until *after* 100.[4]

In 1939, excavations at Herculaneum brought to light the very clear impress of a cross on one of the walls of a Roman patrician's villa – in the slaves' quarters. Around the impress of the cross, the nails which supported either the cross itself or the screen which concealed it were still intact. The villa had been engulfed in the famous eruption of Vesuvius in the year 79. So by then Christianity had spread as far as southern Italy and become firmly established there.

In 1968, under the floor-paving of a Capernaum church (dedicated to Peter since the fifth century and the oldest known in Palestine) came the discovery of what archaeologists are agreed in identifying as Peter's own house. It is a very humble dwelling, no different from the ones around it except that the walls are covered with frescoes and writings (in Greek, Aramaic and Latin) invoking Peter and requesting his protection. There is proof that the house was turned into a 'holy place' as early as the first century, so it is the oldest known Christian 'church'. Moreover it testifies to the fact that before the year 100 not only was worship of Jesus firmly established but also at least one of his disciples was a 'canonised' saint whose protection was invoked.

Returning to the kerygma: is it really in the least likely that a character was 'invented', when 60 years earlier that same character had been linked (in the tradition received by Paul) with a series of verifiable historical events to which witnesses still living could testify?

The kerygma (but not only the kerygma) has undermined the untenable theories of the mythologists just as, together with our knowledge of the Jewish milieu, it has demolished the equally untenable theories of the critical school.

'In the beginning was the kerygma' (Dibelius), and it is this which shows that the Christian message was entire from the start. The Jesus of history and the Christ of faith were one and the same from the earliest years. This is not a pious hope entertained by credulous and indiscriminating believers but a solid fact that has now been proved historically by 'sceptics'.

IV ENGELS AND VOLTAIRE

The Soviet line

We earlier referred to the way philosophy has carried more weight than history for many who have attempted to explain Christianity; that, and the consequent acceptance of pseudo-scientific presuppositions, has had an incalculable effect on the history of the modern world.

A case in point is the Marxist theory on the origins of the Christian faith now offical in the USSR. Engels (surprisingly, in view of his lucid and rational mind) wandered off and got lost in a type of theorising quite unworthy of a scholar of his ability; and for many years Soviet scholars obstinately rejected the findings of the western critics – even when these too were inimical to the Church – so as not to find themselves contradicting Engels. Very recently a little tentative 'self-criticism' has crept into Soviet biblical study; but as late as the early 1960s some articles in the *Great Soviet Encyclopedia* on Christianity and its origins caused considerable embarrassment to Marxist-oriented western scholars when they were published in an Italian translation.

Engels saw the birth of Christianity as a typical example of a revolutionary solution in a class-struggle situation – the slave class on the one side and their oppressors on the other. In his view the new faith has its place in history as 'the religion of slaves and freedmen, the poor and those with no rights, the peoples subjugated and driven out of their homelands by Rome'. In fact 'a movement started by the oppressed classes who, despairing of any material redemption, looked for a substitute in the form of some spiritual redemption'. Belief in a Saviour Christ therefore arose as a perfectly natural development in the proletarian milieux of the eastern Mediterranean, without any real 'founder' as its basis of origin. Karl Kautsky, the most authoritative interpreter of the classic Marxist position, sums it up: 'Christianity is nothing but the mythical expression of a collective force.'

In order to justify this theory of the spontaneous gestation of Christianity, Engels asserted that the gospel of John and the book of Revelation, the latest books of the New Testament, were in fact the first to be written; especially in Revelation did there blow a wind of rebellion and protest against imperial Rome.

As the years went by, Soviet scholars found it more and more difficult to swallow this theory – critics in the west having proved that Revelation and John's gospel were the last of the New Testament books to be written.

Another of Engels's key theories was just as clearly untenable. According to him 'the true doctrinal father of Christianity' was Philo of Alexandria, the first-century Jewish philosopher who tried to effect a synthesis between Judaism and Greek philosophy. How Philo's philosophical writings came to be popularised and known to the poorer classes throughout the Mediterranean Engels failed to state; he simply presupposed that they did – on no evidence whatsoever. But even he was forced to admit that it was difficult to understand why, if Christianity derived from Philo's writings, 'the New Testament almost completely overlooks its fundamentals'.

More and more of Engels's theories were shown to be nonsensical as modern scientific studies of all kinds progressed. For example, his contention that the new faith's 'main centre' of growth was not Palestine but Alexandria or some other place where there was a Jewish community of the diaspora; or his assertion that primitive Christianity met with resounding success because the common people welcomed 'a religion without rites or ceremonies'. Moreover it is now generally accepted that primitive Christianity was by no means confined to the proletariat, as the 'revolutionary' theory would require. Pliny the Younger, writing to Trajan in 112 about the Christians in Bythinia, said they included people *omnis ordinis*, of every social class, adding that 'this superstition has infected not only the cities but also the villages and countryside'. The lists of martyrs in the early centuries include the names of traders, craftsmen, intellectuals and – quite often – well-born landowners. Marcello Craveri, though himself a scholar with Marxist leanings, has no hesitation in saying that until 1958 'USSR scholars approached the problem of the origins of Christianity more concerned to justify Engels's opinions on the subject than to evaluate objectively the fresh data provided by New Testament exegesis, archaeological discovery and the study of ancient history.'

Only after 1958 (publication date of an essay by Kovalev 'in perfect conformity with Marxist thought but free of excessive attachment to the opinions of Engels') did Soviet biblical criticism achieve a degree of scientific credibility.

But self-criticism had to wait until 1968, when the historian Kublanov published a book on New Testament research and the discoveries it had led to. This was favourably reviewed by the authoritative Moscow periodical *Novy Mir* which, after recognising that 'the historical existence of Jesus is a fact that Soviet atheism will have to take into account from now on', ends somewhat surprisingly:

'Between 1920 and 1940 atheist propaganda followed a false trail by slavishly adopting the ideas of bourgeois anti-clericalism which deny the historical existence of Jesus.'

But the real culprit was Engels, with his wild presuppositions; not any deviations dating back only to the Stalinist era.

Kublanov's work marked the beginning of a really new Soviet approach to the study of Jesus. Engels's hypotheses are now for the most part abandoned, and their untenability admitted, by a number of Marxist scholars – although the latest edition of the *Great Soviet Encyclopedia* still takes the old official line that Jesus never so much as existed. But now the Soviet specialists are running into all the problems encountered by German and French biblical criticism in the early part of the twentieth century – all the problems we have discussed in this chapter.

The course of Soviet study of Christianity's origins points a moral. But we would do well not to overlook the fact that no less blasphemous caricatures of Jesus have been drawn in the west in order to use him as an instrument of anti-communist propaganda. Which all goes to show how difficult it is to approach the problem with genuine objectivity.

Bourgeois 'reason' and gospel discrepancies

Lest it be thought that the only clear brain to go astray was that of Engels, that excellent example of socialist rationalism, let us now glance at the aberrations of Voltaire, that perfect example of bourgeois rationalism.

François Marie Arouet, known as Voltaire, enjoys the reputation of 'master of logic, unrivalled unmasker of all the falsities of Christianity, standard-bearer of reason in the battle against biblical obscurantism'. Let us look at what his logic has to say, in his *Dictionnaire Philosophique*, about the genealogy of 'Joseph, the husband of Mary who gave birth to Jesus'.

Whereas Matthew lists only 42 antecedents of Joseph, Luke gives 56; and the names listed in Matthew do not even tally exactly with those given by Luke. And even if they do coincide in places, what makes matters worse is that Luke works backwards to Adam whereas Matthew starts with Abraham and works forwards. A more clumsy pastiche is impossible to imagine, remarks Voltaire in conclusion; how can one regard texts which begin like that as even remotely reliable historically?

Let us be clear straightaway that no Christian scholar, not even the most diehard traditionalist, would attempt to prove that these 'genealogies' are to be considered 'true' in the historical sense; they have a purpose, but that purpose is literary, symbolic and above all theological. But Voltaire and his like seize on them in order to demonstrate that what tradition tells us about Jesus was freely manipulated or wholly invented by believers themselves. They might just as easily have picked on other discrepancies between the different gospels.

Although the many discrepancies that undoubtedly can be found very seldom affect fundamental issues in the interpretation of Jesus's life, the Church was uncomfortably aware of them long before Voltaire. As early as about 150 an unknown Syrian wrote the so-called 'gospel of Peter' in an attempt to eliminate them; but the Church deemed it apocryphal. Towards 170 another writer, Tatian, tried to do the same thing in the text known as the *Diatessaron.* As for Marcion and his contention that one text only should be accepted by the Church, that of Luke for preference, the Church preferred schism rather than acceptance of his view, logical though it seemed.

However, Voltaire's reasoning is curious to say the least.

On the one hand he maintains – as do all the 'scientific' experts who set out to demolish the historicity of the gospels – that these texts are fanciful fiction, built on a basis of legend by a community of believers who wanted a God who would fit in with their expectations, aspirations and beliefs.

On the other hand he and his followers believe that this myth-making community first of all constructed, and then meticulously preserved, texts that clearly fail to agree with one another in a number of details. According to them, the Church so enjoyed making difficulties for herself and laying herself open to attack from unbelievers that she deliberately invented, circulated and preserved intact texts that clearly invited criticism on grounds of inconsistency. ... Voltaire seems not to have noticed how absurd such behaviour on the part of the Church would have been if, as he asserts, there was nothing in the first place on which to build except legend, which could be manipulated at will.

Why did the Church not bow to those second-century objections to the inconsistencies in the gospel accounts? We know that the four gospels we now have, the ones chosen by the Church at just about that time, went through a number of stages before being given their final form; why (given that Jesus himself had left nothing in writing) were they not subjected to a last editing process that would have ironed out all the discrepancies and produced four texts that in no way conflict with one another? That would no doubt have been logical; and it would have facilitated the Church's missionary task. But the Church did not see it that way. Why?

The only possible explanation seems to be that the believing community felt itself under an *obligation* to accept those four texts, embarrassingly inconsistent though they were, and only those four. An obligation that must have had its roots in a reasoned conviction that those texts contained what was remembered by the most reliable witnesses. People's memories were sometimes in disagreement on certain points, and sometimes confused (were the two demoniacs cured near Gadara, as Matthew states, or near Gerasa, as Luke and Mark have it?), but they surely must have been considered the most reliable among the many available testimonies to what did occur.

It is precisely the variations in the four 'official' accounts which lead one to think that in the beginning a genuinely historical life was lived by Jesus, and that in order to piece together the evidence for it there was a need to seek out and preserve the most reliable testimonies to it, those that corresponded most closely to the facts. And these particular testimonies were evidently considered irreproachable.

To the early Church logic and convenience seem to have mattered little, because for the purposes of successful preaching the gospels say both too much and too little. If the early Church was foolish enough to face the world armed with texts that were open to immediate objection, the only explanation for such foolishness must be that in the beginning there was a message which was not open to manipulation at will by the believing community – no matter what the critics and mythologists may say to the contrary. The community appears to have made every effort to ascertain as best it could exactly what happened. And to receive, preach and preserve the message as far as possible intact.

Let us glance again at those genealogies which Voltaire

saw as proof that the gospels are totally unreliable historically. The philosopher's brilliant intelligence failed to notice something that one of his compatriots, R. L. Bruckberger, has pointed out today. Matthew includes the names of four women, besides Mary, in his impeccably constructed list of Jesus's forbears. But this is nonsensical: in the Jewish tradition women did not count at all in genealogies; therefore this one for Jesus was invalidated from the start. Women were creatures to be looked upon with some suspicion, often regarded as 'unclean'; since their very names cast a shadow, such names were totally out of place in any serious geneaology.

Moreover, Jesus is not made to come from priestly stock: he is not said to descend from the tribe of Levi. Why, if the apostles were so full of gratuitous invention, is Jesus not presented with a valid genealogy and one that would provide him with first-class credentials? Any number of similar questions could be asked. Why, for instance, did the myth-makers not give their hero a distinctive name, a name fit for a legendary hero, instead of giving him one of the commonest names there was in Israel at that time?

The fact that no such embroidery is to be found in the gospels tends to support the argument that those who preached about this Messiah were certainly not free to indulge in fanciful invention.

They were not free to do so for one very simple reason: Jesus was being declared to have risen from the dead, and to be Israel's Messiah, in a hostile environment (in Palestine where the events in question had taken place, or in Jewish communities abroad which were in close contact with the motherland) immediately after his death – and publicly into the bargain. The implications of this state of affairs have been largely overlooked by many critics.

V IN PERSPECTIVE

Too much and too little

Let us try to broaden our view of the New Testament documents and see them in perspective, setting them in the historical context which gave rise to them instead of examining little scraps of them under a microscope. We shall then find that the assumption common to both critics and mythologists ('Christianity sprang from a community with a vivid imagination') runs into considerable difficulties, logical as well as historical.

And we shall find that these texts manage to escape being caught in any of the nets spread by their detractors.

The gospels are over-talkative at times when common-sense would require them to say nothing at all. And yet they were the material used by missionaries who called on their hearers to believe the unbelievable simply on the strength of what they themselves said.

These preachers, whose need for their hearers' trust was perhaps greater than that of anyone else in history, went to great lengths to let people know about the jealousy, intrigue, envy, disbelief, small-mindedness, cowardice and lack of understanding that were rife among them during their master's lifetime.

Do the gospels as we now have them reflect the Church's earliest preaching? That they do is one of the least disputed findings of the critical school. Well then, surely, since these texts derive from what was publicly preached, they ought to be different: surely they ought to pass over in silence things that might be better left unsaid. Instead here is a community that lays its credibility open to question from the start, even though it has taken upon itself a missionary task that looks extremely daunting.

The world is called upon to accept some very difficult teaching from men who freely advertise the fact that they themselves couldn't stay awake even for an hour with their master, that they fled when he was in danger and left him to die alone. Disciples who recount how they were often taken to task by their master because they failed to understand the inner meaning of his teaching or because they distorted it. Disciples who appeal to others to have faith and yet depict themselves as deficient in faith to the end.

The unfavourable light deliberately cast on itself by the early community shows up Peter in particular. Leaving aside all the disputes about the value of the primacy Jesus conferred on him, there is no denying that the early Church tended to centre around Peter; in the New Testament he is unquestionably at its head as a 'pillar of faith'. Yet this key figure is depicted in the gospels as 'of little faith', untrustworthy to the point of three times denying all connection with his master. And this he did (not under searching interrogation by the Jewish supreme tribunal but – most shameful of all – in the hearing of a group of servants warming themselves around a night-time fire) at the very time when his master was facing his greatest suffering, his Passion.

Several ingenious theories have been advanced to explain away this incident as an invention, but none of them is convincing. The most reasonable explanation for its inclusion in the gospels is that the early preaching had no option but to refer to even the most embarrassing of incidents; that it was obliged to do so because it was proclaiming news of recent events in a Palestine where there was no lack of opponents ready to challenge any departure from the truth about what had taken place. If the apostles and the early community had strayed even a short way from the truth in what they taught and wrote down, they would themselves have dug the Church's grave.

Such was the situation (for which history provides ample

evidence) when the gospels were beginning to take shape. What conclusions are to be drawn from all this?

One is that in all probability the content of the preaching that went to make up the gospels was subjected to scrutiny by critics far more severe than the modern critical schools. Critics like Israel's Supreme Sanhedrin, not to mention the innumerable eye-witnesses. Therefore there is nothing unreasonable about the 'belief hypothesis' that these texts contain history that is 'true' and not arbitrarily moulded or manipulated, even though they are not factual comptes-rendus in the modern sense of the word.

Moreover, only if their historicity is acknowledged can one explain why the gospels contain both too much and too little.

Peter's denial will serve as an example. If that indeed occurred in public, better surely to talk about it than try to cover it up. Less harm would ensue from referring to it openly than from leaving it to be exposed by some ill-wisher. Those who heard Peter deny being a disciple of the condemned man were servants in the household of the High Priest, Jesus's principal enemy, and they would certainly have reported the incident to him.

As a matter of interest we may note that these details which could so easily embarrass the apostles are found only in the first three gospels, those which most accurately reflect the early preaching. John's gospel shows the disciples in a more favourable light and omits the incidents that depict them as lacking faith and understanding; but it was composed much later, when there was little need (after the fall of Jerusalem and the destruction of the temple) to be wary of what could be disclosed by ill-wishers.

If the theory of 'obligatory' historicity is not accepted, how else can one explain why the gospels record sayings and actions by Jesus which could immediately place a severe strain on his credibility as universal Messiah?

For instance, this Christ is made to say (in Mark and

Matthew) that he does not know when the time will come for his own return and 'the End of the World'. It is a disconcerting admission of ignorance that has bothered many theologians ever since.

Then, in chapter 10 of Matthew, the Christ is said to have sent his disciples out on their mission with the injunction: "*Do not go into pagan territory or into any Samaritan town. Go rather to the lost sheep of the house of Israel.*" Hardly the sort of instruction to go down well with Paul's foreign audiences (and certainly not one to support the theory that the gospels were written in non-Jewish circles).

And in Mark, chapter 10, a young man calls Jesus "*Good master*" and Jesus replies "*Why do you call me good? No one is good except God alone.*" Does this support the theory that the whole text was devised in order to pass a man off as God?

And how else can one explain why the preaching included the assertion that Jesus reserved his first risen appearance for some women? What sort of proof was that, when nobody in Israel attributed any sort of value to the testimony of women? Even the disciples (according to Luke) were highly sceptical of what they reported. And the same scepticism has continued down the ages: according to Renan, faith in the resurrection originated in nothing more than hallucinations on the part of a few hysterical females.

And why is Jesus's degrading death recorded as having taken place in public, in a prominent place and at a time when Jerusalem was at its fullest for the Passover, whereas his glorious resurrection is declared to have occurred secretly, within a tomb during the dark of night? From the second-century onwards there has never been any lack of critics to point out that none of his opponents ever saw him risen.

Several of the apocryphal gospels (which certainly are the product of religious invention) do speak of a Jesus who, having conquered death, went along to strike terror into the Jews who had condemned him. But the mere fact that the canonical gospels choose the way of discretion, recording only appearances to his friends, is in itself a good indication that they by contrast are truthful – the end-product of scrupulous preservation and not of creative invention.

A script with troublesome gaps

If by saying too much the gospels hindered the early community's missionary expansion, by saying too little they put at risk the Church's very existence.

We know for certain that, almost as soon as it came out into the open, the group which preached Jesus risen from the dead had to find the answers to some very real questions. Was it to continue to observe the Jewish religious customs? Must non-Jewish converts be circumcised? Was the preaching to be extended to people of non-Jewish race? Was the sabbath still to be kept as a day of rest? What authority was to be acknowledged in the leaders of the community? How was worship to be organised?

These were pressing questions affecting the whole life and organisation of this little group that was setting out to change the world. They needed to be answered clearly and immediately, but in fact they gave rise to painful internal dissension. From the very earliest days Christianity has been subject to schisms and heresies, which have arisen precisely because the teaching of Jesus, as preached and then preserved in the gospels, is less than comprehensive and less than clear on a number of points.

The Acts of the Apostles and the letters of Paul, Peter, James, John and Jude all expose to the light of day arguments and controversies involving differing theological trends. Yet these same texts show that all the contenders sought to justify their views by claiming the support of this or that saying of Jesus as recorded – even though the particular sayings are equivocal or vague, quite inadequate in practice for settling the questions in dispute.

Why, if this teaching was arbitrarily devised by the community, was the imaginary master made to remain silent about matters that were vital? If all his sayings were fabrications, why were none inserted to eliminate all schism and heresy?

The burning question of 'circumcision or no circumcision' for non-Jewish converts was of such immense importance that after much bitter controversy (reported in Acts and in Paul's letter to the Galatians) it led to the convening of the first Council of Jerusalem. Here there is no question of 'discovering' a verse, or just a word or two, from the lips of the master; instead a solution is sought by appealing to the spirit (not the non-existent letter) of his teaching. Every effort is made to discern what is implicit in his thinking, and to develop what is implicit to meet the demands of fresh and unexpected circumstances. The same is true of the early Church's handling of other controversial issues.

Yet there was nothing to prevent the 'discovery' of new sayings of Jesus. No ill-wishers were in any position to declare that he had never said this or that in private to his apostles – or even to just one of them. So once again we are bound to conclude that the community was scrupulously careful to put its trust exclusively in testimony that it deemed reliable – testimony from those who had themselves seen and heard or had been reliably informed by eye-witnesses; and that what was remembered and recorded by them was considered final, for ever immutable.

The inexplicable silences

The gospels are silent on other matters too. And these silences are inexplicable not only in the context of religious mythology but also from the point of view of Christian psychology – at least as it has become evident down the centuries. Let us look at three examples.

First: Jesus's physical appearance. There is surely no need to point out how much western art (and African and eastern art too) has been almost obsessed with the physical appearance of Jesus: he has been portrayed in every conceivable way. Quite apart from the Holy Shroud of Turin (considered authentic by many scientists who are not Christians, although some Catholic scientists counsel prudence) which becomes more and more fascinating as more becomes known about it, there seem to be thirty-nine other shrouds, cloths, sheets, etc., that have been venerated because they have been thought to bear 'the true image of the face (or body) of Jesus'. But it is now certain that all thirty-nine are pious fakes. From its earliest days Christian faith has tried to reconstruct the features of its God: the apocryphal gospels, and some very early letters later found to be fakes, contain many imaginary descriptions of him.

But in the gospels accepted by the Church there is not a single word about the physical appearance of Jesus. Nothing to arouse devotion or curiosity. Nothing.

This reticence would be inexplicable if the gospels were really imaginary compositions based on a few true facts embroidered with much legend. No other myth or religious epic omits to give frequent descriptions of its hero. Why should the gospels alone be so laconic?

Second: Jesus is recorded as having read the Scriptures aloud in the synagogue at Capernaum. But there is no clear gospel evidence as to whether or not he was able to write as well as read. There is only one vague reference to his 'writing' – in the sand, when he saved the adulterous woman from being stoned by her censorious accusers – but here the possibility that he did not write so much as trace symbolic signs cannot be excluded.

It is surely strange that nothing is said about the schooling and cultural qualifications of a claimant to messiahship in a Jewish world where culture alone carried weight. This particular gospel silence does not suggest that the texts arose out of fideistic distortion or myth.

Third: The four gospels say nothing at all about at least nine-tenths of Jesus's life. Between his birth and the beginning of his preaching only one episode is recorded – his slipping away from his parents at the age of 12 in order to talk to the doctors of the Law in the temple of Jerusalem. Now, if this story was a pious invention those who invented it started off on the wrong foot; for in those days the family and filial obedience were sacred values. Moreover the story showed both Jesus and his parents in a bad light, he because he flouted parental authority and they because they didn't even realise he was missing until the following day.

The writers of the apocryphal gospels didn't hesitate to fill in the gaps with stories well calculated to delight and astonish; but the Church would have none of them.

In point of fact the apocryphal gospels are perfectly in line with religious mythology the world over. Only the four gospels recognised as canonical by the Church fail to fit the pattern required by the mythological school of thought – or into that required by the critical school either.

But here again the third hypothesis, the belief hypothesis, has a ready explanation. The gospels arose out of an intense urge to proclaim the 'good news', the best news there had ever been. "We proclaim your death, Lord Jesus; we proclaim your resurrection, and we await your return in glory": to make that known was what mattered to the apostles. Their main aim was to be heralds of the kerygma: the passion, death and resurrection *for us* of the long-awaited Messiah.

All the rest, for those who propagated the faith and therefore for the gospels which contain their preaching, was secondary if not beside the point. The colour of his eyes, the shape of his beard, his technical and cultural qualifications – what did such details matter when one was bursting to talk about the man in whom God had revealed himself as the one who saves us? The only thing that mattered was telling as many people as possible that he had endured great suffering and had died, but that he had finally conquered death and with it the world and sin; and that we too therefore are saved.

By their very lack of details that could excite facile curiosity the gospels seem to underpin their own veracity and confirm that what was preached stemmed from one traumatic experience – probably the sight of the risen Christ.

Anyone who asserts that a bare-bones text like that of Mark is a heap of myth ought to recognise that it breaks all the rules of imaginative religious literature. And it breaks all the psychological rules too; for anyone unsure of himself piles up his supporting evidence, whereas anyone quietly confident of the truth of what he is saying sees no need to elaborate on the simple straightforward facts.

This emphasis on the message itself, this concentration on basics – on the mystery of Easter – could even explain the discrepancies between the individual gospels. The texts were produced for the sole purpose of spreading belief in a Messiah whom men rejected but whom God highly exalted. Geography and topography, flora and fauna, political and social history were of concern to the preachers only to the extent that they formed the necessary framework for the actions and teachings of this risen Christ.

A solid corpus of recollections preserved by a hierarchically structured group

The early Church considered herself in duty bound to maintain the 'deposit of faith' intact, acting not as its master but as its custodian and faithful administrator. If proof of this is needed it can be found in Paul.

Paul very probably never knew Jesus during his lifetime or saw or heard what he said and did. Despite feeling that he had been entrusted with a privileged revelation on the road to Damascus, he was anxious that his preaching should in no respect differ from that of those who certainly were, as he put it, 'witnesses according to the flesh'.

When he learned that some trouble-makers among the Galatians had been spreading doubts about what he had preached to them, he wrote them an impassioned letter going straight to the point: '*After three years I went up to Jerusalem to visit Cephas (Peter) and stayed with him for fifteen days. ... Then, after fourteen years I went up to Jerusalem again, with Barnabas, and taking Titus with me too. I went there as a result of a revelation, and privately I laid before the leading men the Gospel I preach among the pagans – for fear the course I was adopting or had adopted might not be approved. ... These people who are the acknowledged leaders had nothing to add to the Gospel as I preach it.*'

Thus even in Paul's eyes – and he was fully conscious of his own privileged position – his preaching was authoritative because it had been approved by those whose testimony was based on their own personal recollections. It was those personal recollections that determined what was or was not 'authentic' preaching; and that was the position by the year 40, for the letter to the Galatians was written not later than 57. No preacher was at liberty to add or subtract anything without the approval of the 'leading men' then still in Jerusalem. '*If anyone preaches a version of the Gospel different from the one we have preached to you – be it ourselves or an angel from heaven – let him be condemned*' (Paul's letter to the Galatians).

In scrupulous adherence to a message fixed once and for all by the recollections of eye-witnesses, Paul distinguishes with great care between the clearly expressed will of his Lord and his own personal opinions. In the seventh chapter of his first letter to the Corinthians: '*To the married man there is something to be said – and this is not from me but from the Lord: a wife must not leave her husband.*' Up to that point Paul has merely been giving 'advice' based on his own religious sensibilities, but then he adverts to a precise saying of Jesus remembered by those who had heard him speak. Later he makes it quite clear that what he writes next is his own opinion only. And there are many other examples, both in Paul's letters and those of other apostles, of this careful distinction between personal opinion and immutable sayings of the Lord. Does this suggest the sort of free-for-all medley that so many scholars would have us believe the New Testament to be?

Leaving aside the many theories that owe more to philosophical pressures than to well-documented historical realities, the fact is that from the start of her history the Church was a hierarchically structured group of people, not in the least unruly and loquacious, ungovernable and at the mercy of its emotions, as the critics and mythologists like to pretend.

As early as the year 40, history had to deal with a small but carefully regulated community under the control of 'leading men', the apostles. And they in their turn are shown to have been subordinate to a 'head', Cephas, the 'rock' Peter, who monitored their words and their actions.

The history of this group begins with the problem of finding a substitute for Judas. What criterion governs the choice of a new member of the 'committee' of twelve which safeguards the faith that is preached? The criterion is laid down by Peter, according to the Acts of the Apostles: "*We must choose someone from among those who were with us all the time Jesus was with us, from the time when John was baptising until the day he was taken up from us; and he can act with us as a witness to his resurrection.*" Matthias was 'numbered among the twelve' apostles because he had been close to Jesus throughout his mission – not because he had shown himself able to enunciate prophecy while in a state of trance, or to speak unknown languages in tones of evident inspiration. ... That sort of criterion would certainly justify the contentions of those who assert that the Christian community was a collection of fanatics; but it was not the criterion laid down by Peter.

A matter of style

The critics and mythologists have yet another hurdle to negotiate. How do they explain why in the gospel texts there is no relation between *content* and *form* (if such a distinction is permissible)? Why, if these texts sprang from a fideistic hysteria that went to the lengths of turning a man into a god or attributing a body to a mythical saviour-god, are they written in a style that is so inimical to those hypotheses?

Martinetti, one of the later disciples of the critical school, imagines an atmosphere in which hysterical hallucination was a commonplace: 'The first Christian community was a community of enthusiasts with its own inspired orators, its own prophets. At its meetings ecstatic utterances, glossolalia, were a frequent phenomenon, and the glossolalia were normally accompanied by visions, prophecies and miracles.'

Would such a crowd of delirious gabblers have expressed its beliefs in texts like the canonical gospels, the style of which is aptly described by the specialists as 'gospel impassiveness'?

Neither in the content nor in the style of these texts is there anything redolent of fake or hysteria. Quite the reverse.

The gospel-writers indulge in no shouts of exultation at the birth of their Messiah, nor do they give vent to loud lamentation at his death.

Instead they invariably show the detachment of the objective reporter: the bare facts only are given, with scarcely ever so much as a comment stressing this one or that. They are more the stuff of news bulletins than of legend. The most striking thing about them, after their impassiveness, is their naturalness of expression. There is no lofty rhetoric. This man about whom such extraordinary things are recounted is described in the language and images of everyday life. What emerges is the portrait of a genuine person whom prejudice alone can turn into a phantom-figure in some myth.

And this down-to-earthness persists even after the resurrection. John's gospel shows us the man who overcame death on the cross cooking fish over a fire at the lakeside in the early morning mist. 'We would have expected to see Jesus, after the Resurrection and just before the Ascension, making very different preparations for his last meeting with his apostles' (Tournier).

'We would have expected ...'. Yes; if it were all a myth we certainly would. But the gospels give the clear impression that they are true recollections of a man who had in fact been seen eating bread and olives, getting angry and then rejoicing, laughing and crying. A man who had actually been heard to snore during the night. ...

The accounts flow on against a background 'that brings to life a corner of the Palestine countryside with all its comings and goings, its fishing and its harvests, funerals and weddings, children, friends and enemies, the yearly cycle of the seasons' (Karl Barth).

Anyone glancing through the three synoptic gospels can see for himself what we are trying to convey. Even the most breath-taking miracles are recorded in matter-of-fact terms. And they certainly do not look like interpolations made later to satisfy faith. 'An attempt made to strip the gospels of the miracles has shown that if this is done the texts become disconnected, the narrative breaks up and the argument no longer makes any sense' (Albanese).

The ordinary and the extraordinary are so closely bound up with one another that the reaction of anyone who doesn't skate around the problem is that *either* these texts have to be accepted en bloc *or else* they have to be rejected no less en bloc. The solid rock of the gospels is so resistant that to split it into 'authentic happenings' and 'fideistic accretions' is utterly impossible.

Here again, comparison with the apocryphal gospels settles the argument. In them we find the unmistakable style of mythical invention. Here there is everything that is not to be found anywhere in the gospels accepted by the Church as her own: miracles to no purpose, useless miracles narrated simply in order to astound the reader; rapturous descriptions of a baby Jesus who models little birds out of clay and then breathes on them to infuse life into them and make them fly; or whose omnipotence enables his mother to draw water from the well without the assistance of any mechanism to wind up the bucket. Here indeed is the unmistakable odour of myth and legend.

The apocrypha writers give themselves away because they ask too much of faith. They make no distinction between the supernatural and the merely astonishing. The canonical gospel-writers never succumb to that temptation: the miracles they recount are simply 'signs' which support or confirm the truth of the teaching.

Moreover, the most sober in tone of all the gospels is the oldest one, Mark. Now, if in the first place there was merely an explosion of religious feeling that turned an obscure preacher into God, the oldest of the gospels ought surely to reflect that original outburst of wild enthusiasm and contain more that looks like legend; and the later texts ought to provide evidence of some sifting process designed to rid the faith of primitive 'excesses'. But this is not the case: the last to be written, John, is not content with the facts the others have narrated but adds theological reflection about them.

Even the accounts of the institution of the Eucharist are subject to the gospel-writers' strict self-control; the supreme expression of the Church's faith is described as having been instituted in the course of an otherwise unremarkable meal; there were no visions, no mysterious phenomena, no claps of thunder or flashes of light. And the resurrection, the very foundation of the faith, is dealt with by Mark in no more than a few matter-of-fact verses.

Notes

1 In the Acts of the Apostles, chapter 5, we read how the disciples of Jesus were hauled before the Jewish Sanhedrin to be condemned to death. But Gamaliel, a member of the Sanhedrin and '*a pharisee, a doctor of the Law and highly thought of by all the people*', cautioned his colleagues, reminding them of what had become of two pseudo-messiahs and advising them to '*leave these men alone and set them free; because if this enterprise, this movement, is of human origin it will break up of its own accord; but if it is of God you will not be able to suppress it*'.

2 For instance they also overlooked the fact that any ordinary Jew who had said 'Drink my blood' would have been stoned on the spot. One of the most rigorous of Judaism's taboos has always been the one enjoining abstention from blood. According to chapter 15 of the Acts of the Apostles, this injunction was one of the few 'essentials' of Judaism that the first Council of Jerusalem decided must be retained. This is just one piece of evidence that the gospel teaching was certainly not 'invented' by the Christian community; it suggests, rather, that the community found itself faced with having to accept teaching which in a number of respects was upsetting, even blasphemous.

3 Some other attempts to explain the inexplicable are quite laughable. Proudhon in his later years admitted that the transition from the Jesus of history to the Christ of faith was impossible to account for if the master did die on the cross; therefore he did not; instead he was taken down from it alive, brought back to consciousness and then, when restored to health, remained in hiding and clandestinely guided the activities of his followers until the year 70. ... Another rationalist, Paulus, decided that Jesus came out of the sepulchre alive, dressed himself in the gardener's clothes and pretended to Mary Magdalen that he had risen from the dead; then he went off to Emmaus in order to deceive the other two disciples; subsequently he practised the same deception in Galilee before dying of tetanus, contracted through the wounds made by the nails. ...

4 Apropos ancient copies of the New Testament, it is generally agreed by specialists in such matters that 'none of the books of antiquity has been transmitted with so much accuracy and in so many ancient manuscripts as the New Testament' (Thiel). At least 4,680 distinct copies, including about 60 on papyrus, have now been identified. P 66, published in 1966, contains the full text of John's gospel; it is dated around 150.

8.

Myth and history

Let us suppose that historians living in the third millennium come across a short biography of Napoleon – one of the few documents to survive the atomic holocaust that almost destroyed civilisation. If they apply to it the methods that have been applied to the documents about Jesus, they will prove that Napoleon was a purely mythical figure, the hero of a legend in which 19th century man incarnated the pre-existing idea of 'The Great Military Leader'.

The Egyptian and Russian expeditions, the island birth and death, the name itself, the betrayal, fall, resurrection and final downfall brought about by envy and the forces of reaction, the mid-ocean exile – 'all this makes it perfectly clear that Napoleon never existed. We have here the eternal myth of "the Emperor" – perhaps the idea of France itself – given a fictitious name and fictitious exploits by an obscure group of fanatical patriots active early in the 19th century'. So the world will be told by any number of experts – the successors of the scholars who apply this method to the problem of Jesus.

JEAN GUITTON

A fake picture in a genuine frame?

We have been looking at some of the more obvious contradictions in the theories of the critical and mythological schools of thought concerning the origins of Christianity, and also at some of the more serious objections to those theories. Until now we have concentrated on considerations that need to be taken into account by the critics in particular; it is now time to look at a few other matters which ought to concern the mythologists more directly.

If the critics still have no satisfactory answer to the basic question 'How was it possible, in a Jewish milieu, for a mere man to be divinised?', the mythologists for their part have still to answer satisfactorily the question 'How can the events and teaching contained in the gospels be merely legendary when the historical framework in which the "legend" is set has increasingly turned out to be genuine?'

The mythologists' problem has become much more acute in recent decades as our knowledge of ancient Israel has improved, and as science itself has drastically reduced the time-lag without which myth-making is impossible.

If the gospel-writers were fakers, never were there fakers to outdo them. Only the modern masters of the historical novel – Flaubert with his reconstruction of Carthage in *Salammbô*, or Manzoni with his picture of seventeenth-century Lombardy in *I Promessi Sposi* – can rival them.

Obviously no scholar belonging to any of the various mythological schools will begin by presupposing that the gospels were put together by a team of researchers poring over records in libraries, intent on ensuring faultless local colour in the setting for their hero's exploits. On the contrary. Ignoring (to their cost) the historical reality of the early Church, they all take it for granted that the gospels are of anonymous collective authorship, the work of groups of fanatics, of communities carried away by hysteria. And these undefined creative forces are supposed to have given tongue here, there and everywhere in the Mediterranean, the end result being the gospel texts we now have. ...

We have already seen how poorly this supposedly 'scientific' theory accords with the form and content of the gospels. Let us now see how far it fits in with the historical framework that provides the gospel setting.

At the age of 80 Père Lagrange, OP, having spent fifty

years studying in Palestine in order to check every gospel detail against the known facts (local customs, history, archaeology) said: "My work has led me to conclude that there are no sustainable 'technical' objections to the veracity of the gospels. Every detail the texts refer to, when scientifically checked, is found to be accurate." Anyone doubting Père Lagrange's competence should refer to the hundreds of issues of his *Revue Biblique*.

We now come to yet another inconsistency frequently met with in the writings of the devotees of reason.

Nobody disputes that the gospels derive from the preaching of a few 'heralds of the faith' who were concerned above all to proclaim the life, death and resurrection of Jesus; we have seen how everything else, for them, was of secondary importance. Now, the wise 'men of reason' have no esteem whatever for what is the *essential* of these texts – the divinity of Christ; but with a remarkable lack of consistency they accept that what is purely *incidental* in them is completely trustworthy.

Thus, the communities responsible for creating the faith are certainly not to be taken seriously when they talk about Jesus and his miracles, his life and his teaching; but they are fully reliable when they construct a social, geographical and historical framework as the setting for what is supposed to have happened to him.

To tell the truth, the mythologists (and even the critics) would gladly avoid conceding any reliability at all to the gospels, but the results of research and excavations are not to be denied.

Nobody can now dispute that the texts give a perfect description of Jewish–Roman society before the destruction of the temple of Jerusalem in AD 70.

Anyone who gives credence to the mythological hypothesis of undefined creative forces has to explain how, on that basis, the texts manage to give so exact a picture of the most difficult thing of all to reconstruct – society in an occupied country, with all its complex inter-acting authorities and institutions, all its juridical subtleties. The picture that does emerge never ceases to impress precisely because its historical flavour is so very marked.

By the time the gospels took definitive shape that most unusual society had ceased to exist. Unusual it had certainly been for the last hundred years of its existence. Herod the Great ruled only by courtesy of the Romans; on his death in 4 BC the territory was split: Judaea and Samaria went to his son Archelaus as ethnarch (under the tetrarch Philip) and two years later became a procuratorial province, whereas Galilee went to the tetrarch Herod Antipas, a vassal of Rome. And that was only the beginning: there were many more changes of dependency in later years.

The third chapter of Luke's gospel begins by dating the start of Jesus's public ministry. It lists the names of seven religious and political leaders together with their functions; all have been proved to be perfectly correct:

'*In the fifteenth year of Tiberius Caesar's reign, when Pontius Pilate was governor of Judaea, Herod tetrarch of Galilee, his brother Philip tetrarch of Iturea and Trachonitis, Lysanius tetrarch of Abilene, during the pontificate of Annas and Caiphas, the word of God came to John son of Zechariah in the wilderness.* ...'

Against this highly complex background moved the various religious groups – Herodians, Sadducees, Pharisees, followers of John. ... All are identified briefly but precisely.

Irwin Linton, a magistrate of the US Supreme Court and author of a book on the New Testament from a jurist's point of view, has remarked that the type of testimony provided by the gospels corresponds with the norms acceptable to any modern tribunal and to any judge: 'It gives the names, the places and the times.'

Is it at all reasonable to suppose – as the mythologists do – that groups of fanatics living far away in time and space from what is here described in such detail suddenly gave tongue spontaneously to the gospel narratives? For the mythologists assign the writing of these narratives to a period when the society described in them had long since ceased to exist – a time when Israel had been destroyed for decades past, all its institutions gone and even its old place-names replaced by others reflecting a completely new territorial situation, with Jerusalem re-named *Aelia Capitolina* and become forbidden ground for any Jew.

Is it 'scientific' to believe that some half-crazed Syrians, Alexandrians, Cypriots and Antiochenes were capable of depicting with such accuracy, close on half a century after the fall of Jerusalem, the complex interplay of responsibilities and relationships involving the procurator Pontius Pilate and the Jewish Sanhedrin in a case where the death penalty was a distinct anomaly?

Pilate's wife – and some others

On the subject of Pontius Pilate, Matthew tells us that the procurator in Judaea had his wife with him. This detail was much disputed until quite recently, when it was found to be historically valid: shortly before Jesus's time Rome did authorise its representatives to take their families with them to the provinces, a practice previously forbidden.

Other recent discoveries have 'rehabilitated' the Acts of the Apostles, a book much derided in the past by the critics who tried to strip it to the bone.

The author of Acts (Luke, according to a tradition dating back to apostolic times) mentions in chapter 13 the Roman *proconsul* in Cyprus, Sergius Paulus. 'Wrong!' exclaimed the mythologists with delight. Indeed by all normal standards the Roman representative in Cyprus ought to have been a *propraetor*, not a proconsul. But a few years ago an inscription found at Paphos, in the extreme west of the island, names Sergius Paulus – the very man! – as in fact *proconsul.* It is difficult to see how the imaginary fakers of Acts could have got to know of the anomalous title bestowed on that one man.

Even the author of a novelette could hardly have dreamed up the idea of calling the city councillors of Thessalonika *politarchs.* That designation occurs only in this one passage in Acts; it is quite unknown in any other ancient writings. But quite recently excavations have thrown up nineteen inscriptions confirming that in Thessalonika there were indeed officials called *politarchs.*

Guignebert dismissed the wretched author of Acts as patently ill-informed and 'inconsistent'. In point of fact the book is brimful of reliable circumstantial information.

Among other things the author lets us know that at Ephesus (in Roman Asia) those who presided over the imperial cult and public games were called *asiarchs,* and that in the same city the principal municipal dignitary (the town clerk) was known as the *secretary;* that in Jerusalem under the procurator Felix, the *tribune of the cohort* was named Claudius Lysias; that when Paul arrived in the region of Achaia (after AD 44 a senatorial province governed by a proconsul) the *proconsul*'s name was Gallio. Modern historians and archaeologists have found all this – and much more besides – to be completely accurate information.

One more example, from Matthew's gospel again. In chapter 22 Jesus is questioned about the permissibility of paying taxes to the occupying power, Rome:

'*But Jesus, knowing their malice, said: "You hypocrites, why do you try to catch me out? Show me the coins you use to pay the tribute." They handed him a denarius. He said to them: "Whose head is this, and what is the inscription?"; they answered: "Caesar's ..."*.'

The episode has often been scorned as 'impossible' on the grounds that in Israel (where any depiction of the human face was forbidden on pain of death) coins bearing the head of the emperor could never have been in circulation. But history has the last word once again: occupied Palestine was forbidden to strike any but copper coins; those in rarer metals, like the denarius, came direct from the mints in Italy. They bore the head of the emperor, and the occupying power forced the reluctant Jews to accept them.

Time and again history comes down on the side of those 'credulous' believers who accept what is recounted in the New Testament as 'true'.

A challenge to check the facts

The gospels, and the New Testament in general, seem almost to throw down a challenge: "Check what is being preached against facts which are common knowledge!" Accusations of fabrication undoubtedly were not lacking from the very beginning.

Matthew's gospel, the one written for preaching to the Jews, makes the birth of Jesus at Bethlehem coincide with a number of events that had taken place in Israel and were no doubt still remembered by many who heard the message preached: the arrival of the 'magi' which set the whole of Jerusalem talking; the appearance of the brilliant star; Herod's decree that all the male children under two years old in Bethlehem and the surrounding district were to be killed. ...

One may ask why, if the birth in Bethlehem was fictitious and devised simply to fit in with the old prophecy of Micah, was it all made so complicated? Why wasn't Jesus simply made out to have been born in Bethlehem *in secret*?

The same applies to the gospel of Luke, the one which reflects what was preached to the Romans, and the only one to explain why the birth took place in Bethlehem:

'*Now at that time Caesar Augustus issued a decree for a census of the whole world. This census took place before*

Quirinius became governor of Syria. And everyone went to his own town to be registered.'

Thus whereas what was preached to the Jews (Matthew) included references to events known to Jews, what was preached to the Romans (Luke) referred to an event and a person which Romans could easily identify if they chose.

The challenge is discernible in many other gospel accounts; the names and patronymics of person after person are mentioned, as if to call them in as corroborative witnesses.

Why, when narrating the burial of Jesus, not simply mention 'a sepulchre'? Why add details that could – if they were *not* genuine – undermine the credibility of the preaching? The gospel writers clearly had no doubts about the reliability of the details they provided: Luke says that the sepulchre belonged to Joseph, of Arimathea, a *member of the Council* (the Sanhedrin) and therefore one of the best-known men in Jerusalem; Mark adds that Joseph was a *prominent* member of the Council; Matthew adds that he was *wealthy.* As if that were not enough, John brings in Nicodemus alongside Joseph; and Nicodemus had earlier been described as '*one of the Pharisees*' and '*a leading Jew*' (chapter 5).

Jesus was made to carry his own cross. At one point along the road the military escort commandeered a passer-by to relieve him of the burden he was by then incapable of bearing. The man they picked on is not left unidentified: all three synoptic gospels name him as Simon of Cyrene; Luke and Mark both describe him as '*coming in from the country*' outside Jerusalem, and Mark adds that he was '*the father of Alexander and Rufus*'. Excavations in the valley of Cedron, near Jerusalem, brought to light in 1962 a family tomb in a burial-ground dating back to the first century; among other members of the family the inscriptions list an 'Alexandra daughter of Simon' and an 'Alexander of Cyrene'. Pure coincidence? Who can tell? In any case, Alexander and

Rufus were doubtless known to the Roman circle in which Mark wrote his gospel.

Again in Mark, in chapter 10: Jesus came to Jericho and restored the sight of a blind beggar sitting by the side of the road. Once again the man is not left unidentified: he was Bartimaeus, the son of Timaeus.

In the Acts of the Apostles: Peter made his debut as a wonder-worker by healing a man who had been a cripple from birth. No name is given in this case; but none was necessary, for the man was well known in Jerusalem: '*They used to set him down every day near the temple entrance called the Beautiful Gate, so that he could beg from the people going in.*' People used to go in three times a day for public prayer, and the Beautiful Gate was no small side-entrance. Would so familiar a figure have been made the object of Peter's miracle if a check on the facts was in the least likely to show the story up for a fable? The narrative continues: '*everyone recognised him as the man who used to sit begging at the Beautiful Gate of the temple; and they were all astonished and unable to explain what had happened to him*'. A great crowd gathered; Peter seized the opportunity of proclaiming the resurrection of Jesus; priests, temple guards and Sadducees – all furious – arrested him together with John who was with him and held them both in prison overnight; the next day the '*rulers, elders and scribes held a meeting with Annas, the high priest, Caiaphas, John, Alexander and all the members of the high priestly families. ... "What are we to do with these men? ... It is obvious to all Jerusalem that a miracle has been worked through them in public, and we cannot deny it".*'

Any 'inventor' of such an incident would have been foolhardy indeed to present his detractors with so many witnesses to his 'sheer invention'.

There is no point in citing further examples; the New Testament is full of them. They all go to make the mythological hypothesis less and less tenable.

An unexpected end to the 'symbols' guessing-game

According to the mythologists, John's gospel is the ultimate in 'legend', far outstripping in that respect all the other books of that conglomerate of myth known as the New Testament. It is a conviction shared by the critics too. Yet here again recent research has come up with some awkward findings.

Jean Guitton has remarked: 'John's gospel ought to be the least concerned of them all with setting Jesus fairly and squarely in his historical context; for its aim is to lay before us the Word – the Word made flesh but transcending the flesh. Present in time but co-eternal. This gospel dates from the end of the first century, more than two generations later than the facts it narrates. It was intended for the more intellectual disciples, who would be unlikely to care much about personal names or about topographical exactitude in regard to places long forgotten, given that Jerusalem was already destroyed years before it was written. So it is strange that this text is so precise about the dates, the times of day and the itineraries Jesus followed.' For instance it cites at least twenty place-names in Israel not mentioned in the other three gospels.

Excavations in Jerusalem have confirmed that the author of John's gospel knew a great deal more about the city before its destruction than had previously been thought. He shows himself to have a clear picture of what the capital was like in Jesus's day. He mentions several places there which the three synoptics seem unaware of, including the *pool of Bethzatha* and the *Litostrotum.* Startling discoveries of both of these have now been made. Yet both references had been ingeniously interpreted by the mythologists as 'symbol'.

Chapter 5: '*By the Sheep Gate in Jerusalem there is a pool, in Hebrew called Bethzatha, which has five porticos.*'

These few words let loose a flood of mythological speculation. The 'pool with five porticos' was, of course, non-historical. It symbolised the five tribes of Israel; the first five books of the Bible (the Pentateuch); the faculties of the human mind; the five fingers of the hand of Yahweh; the five gates of the Heavenly City. ... Other interpretations tried to draw bold parallels with eastern religions and cults. Any weird and wonderful suggestion was welcome; the only people barred from the guessing-game were those who timidly suggested that perhaps this was a perfectly straightforward recollection of a known place.

Great was the surprise when, just beside one of the old city gates identified as the Sheep Gate, excavations brought to light an extensive bath, about 100 metres long and from 62–80 metres wide (so not quite rectangular) with arcades on all four sides. It had five porticos. The pool of Bethzatha is now marked on the plans of Jerusalem printed for tourists. ... So much for the weighty tomes churned out by the German mythological school!

Chapter 19: '*Pilate had Jesus brought out, and seated himself on the seat of judgment at a place called the Pavement, in Hebrew Gabbatha.*'

What was this place, mentioned only by John? The Greek *litostrotos* certainly means 'a paved area'; the Aramaic *gabbatha* means 'a height'. For centuries nothing was known of the topography of Jerusalem, so the inventors of 'symbols' enjoyed themselves hugely.

But in 1927 the French archaeologist Vincent found the place. It is a paved courtyard of about 2,500 square metres, and the paving is Roman. It is in fact the courtyard of the Antonia, the imperial guard fortress in which the Roman procurator resided during winter and the Passover season. While the Greek term derives from the paving, the Aramaic name is explained by the fact that the Antonia fort was built on the highest of the four hills of ancient Jerusalem.

Nazareth and Pilate

Let us go further afield than John's gospel.

Nazareth, where the evangelists tell us that Jesus spent the years before his public ministry, is never mentioned in the Old Testament. Nor is it mentioned in any of the old Hebrew commentaries on the scriptures. So the mythologists' interpretations of Nazareth, and the adjective *Nazarene*, were many and various; but all assumed that Nazareth was a mythical town with a symbolic name.

In 1962 an Israeli archaeological team led by Professor Avi Jonah of the University of Jerusalem carried out a series of excavations in the ruins of Caesarea, the summer residence of the Roman procurators of Judaea. They came across a grey marble tablet, about 15cm by 12cm, bearing four lines of inscription – in an old Hebrew script certainly not later than the third century BC. Therein was a place-name – Nazareth. So for the first time there was certainty about the town's existence.

But in spite of the fact that this marble tablet from Caesarea has been on display in the Jerusalem archaeological museum for years, theories that ignore its existence persist. Marcello Craveri's *Vita di Gesù*, 'corrected and brought up-to-date' in 1974, informs us that: 'According to many scholars Nazareth never existed.' The appellation 'Nazarene' applied to Jesus in the New Testament 'ought therefore to be related to the Aramaic term *nazirite* applied to those who made a vow, permanent or temporary, of chastity and obedience, and kept their hair uncut for the duration of the vow'. Or, the etymology of Nazarene should be sought in the Syriac term *nasaya* which means 'protected by God'. Or, it derives from *netser* meaning 'branch, shoot, scion'; Matthew's gospel in particular invented a town called Nazareth in order to be able to call its hero a Nazarene and thus prove that he fulfilled the Old Testament prophecy: '*A branch shall come forth from the stem of Jesse and a scion (netser) shall spring from its roots.*' Craveri insists that all these are perfectly legitimate interpretations, given that 'there are no clear indications that a place called Nazareth existed in Jesus's time'. When those lines were written, the third century BC tablet had been on display for twelve years. ...

In the course of the centuries-old debate over the origins of Christianity, doubt has often been cast on Pilate's historicity; references to him by non-Christian writers were dismissed as 'interpolations by Christian copyists'.

In that same museum in Jerusalem there is a limestone tablet, 80cm by 60cm, found at Caesarea in 1961 by an Italian archaeological expedition. Three lines of the inscription are still perfectly clear: '*...S Tiberieum ... tius Pilatus ... ectus Juda ...*'.

Here we have the first indisputable proof not only of the historical existence of Pontius Pilate but also of his praefecture (... *ectus* was originally *praefectus*) in Jesus's time, under Tiberius.

Critic turned mythologist

Greater misfortunes still can befall the critic when for the sake of being up to date he tries to emulate the mythologist and goes running after symbol.

Let us glance at just three examples from poor old Loisy's *Origins of Christianity* – still regarded by some people as the final word in such matters.

On the subject of the burial of Jesus as narrated in the gospels: 'The great stone rolled against the entrance to the sepulchre serves to emphasise the miracle of the resurrection.' This method of entombment, said by the gospels to be normal among the Jews, is made out to be a symbolic invention on the part of persons unknown. Anyone who has read Loisy will therefore be surprised to find, on visiting Abu Gosh north-west of Jerusalem, a whole series of first-century tombs all with great stones rolled against the entrances. The same sort of thing can be seen in many other places in Israel, not forgetting Jerusalem's so-called 'Tomb of the Kings'.

The tomb itself, the evangelists say, was hewn out of the rock. Loisy says: 'Doubtless an invention, to show the prophecies being fulfilled.'

Just over a mile from Jerusalem's Damascus Gate is a place called Shanedrin. There a great many ancient tombs are to be found, all hewn out of the face of the rock. Better still, in the basilica of the Holy Sepulchre the traces of a tomb of the Herodian era hewn out of the rock-face can be seen very close to the point where tradition has always situated the tomb of Jesus. Soundings made in August 1974 showed that the Holy Sepulchre is built on the site of an ancient stone quarry – very suitable as a burial-place for well-to-do people like Joseph of Arimathea.

Loisy quite simply did not know that to situate sepulchres in disused quarries, or to hew them out of the rock-face when no ready-made sites were available, was normal practice in ancient Israel.

He was equally ignorant about other matters to do with burial when he wrote, apropos the '*mixture of myrrh and aloes, weighing about a hundred pounds*' brought by Nicodemus to embalm the corpse, that this was another invention by the evangelist 'to enhance the dignity of the burial and perfect its symbolism'.

Ever since the Holy Shroud of Turin was first photographed in 1898 (and found to bear a perfect negative imprint) there has been much painstaking research into Jewish burial practices in Jesus's time. And it is firmly established that the mixture said to have been brought by Nicodemus was the customary one of aromatics and anti-putrefactants.

Faith does not rest on archaeology

We could go on, but to do so would risk charges of triumphalism. In any case it is perfectly obvious that archaeology does not prove the essential content of scripture – the message of faith. We have already seen that what mattered to the New Testament writers was to broadcast a proclamation of salvation: nothing was further from their thoughts than to compile a guide-book to the 'holy places'.

Archaeology is important to the extent that it can – and has shown that it can – prove the historicity of the framework of the message. The message itself is quite another matter; it will always elude historical proof. As one archaeologist has written with regard to the Old Testament: 'Recent excavations have shown that in the thirteenth century BC a great wave of destruction took place in southern Palestine. That this destruction was caused by the invasion of Palestine by the Jewish people (under Joshua) is a perfectly reasonable historical deduction to make. But that God himself directed the struggle for his own purposes within history (as the biblical writers assert) is an interpretation of faith, susceptible of no proof either historical or archaeological.'

Because it has shown up the weakness of nineteenth- and early twentieth-century attitudes of *a priori* mistrust of the scriptures, the so-called 'archaeological revolution' has rendered an important service. If nothing else it has restored respectability to attitudes of trust in the historicity of the framework – attitudes which were often spurned even as the basis for a mere working hypothesis.

The work goes on; and now, fortunately, much of the heat has gone out of the arguments between textual critics and archaeologists.

For eighteen centuries nobody doubted his existence

All the mythologists' theories have proceeded from the assumption that a man called Jesus cannot be proved to have existed because we have insufficient evidence of him from non-Christian sources. Recent progress in research has some bearing on that basic assumption.

Not so long ago a very ancient document came to light – a letter written in AD 73 by a minor Syrian historian, Mara Bar Sarapion, to his son who was studying in Edessa. Among other things he recalls that the Jews were said to have executed their 'wise king' who had tried to give them new laws. That, according to Bar Sarapion, was why Israel had now undergone punishment in the shape of destruction of the kingdom and massacre and dispersion of the people.

Obviously this letter is not decisive in establishing the historical existence of Jesus. But its date, together with the fact that the writer was certainly not a Christian, shows that within a very few decades of Jesus's death it was generally known in the middle east that a 'King of the Jews', a new lawgiver, had been killed by those who ought to have become his subjects.

This is yet further confirmation that the Christian 'legend', so-called, had taken clear shape long before the end of the first century.

It has to be remembered that until towards the end of the eighteenth century nobody, not even the bitterest enemies of Christianity, dreamed of denying that Jesus had ever existed. Not even the earliest anti-Christian polemicists in whose day the imperial archives were still intact.

Only since the eighteenth century is so much fuss made about the lack of references to him in the ancient sources. But, as one German scholar has pertinently asked, where are all these many Roman histories that have been so vainly searched for references to Jesus? The plain fact is that they do not exist. The only ones extant are those of Tacitus and Suetonius. And both of these do mention him.

Besides Tacitus (about the year 115) and Suetonius (about 120), Pliny the Younger had something to say about the origins of Christianity (towards 112). Earlier still a Samaritan called Thallus, author of a history that seems to have been written in Rome in about the year 60, took issue with the Christians about the nature of the 'darkness over all the land' for three hours while Jesus was dying.

Flavius Josephus spoke of him in his *Jewish Antiquities*, written in about 93. Before discussing the best-known passage (from the *Testimonium Flavianum*) let us glance at an important line referring to the execution of a certain James, whom Josephus calls 'the brother of Jesus, the so-called Christ'. This reference can hardly be a later Christian interpolation: any such interpolation would in all probability have spoken not of the *brother* of Jesus but of a *cousin*, for argument over this matter of 'brothers and sisters of Jesus' was rife in the Church quite early on. And no pious faker would have dreamed of referring to his God as 'the so-called Christ'.

That Josephus did mention Jesus in the passage about the Christian Messiah (the passage in the *Testimonium*) was virtually certain. But in precisely what terms he himself did so was open to question. For the phraseology of the passage was such as to suggest very strongly the hand of a Christian. Josephus was no Christian; yet he spoke of 'Jesus, a wise man, if one can call him a man', and said that 'he worked miracles' and appeared to his disciples 'alive again' three days after his death. Finally: 'He was the Christ.'

Almost all scholars, including Catholics, therefore concluded that a Christian copyist had manipulated the original Josephus text.

In 1971 a decisive discovery was made by Professor Shlomo Pines of the Hebrew University of Jerusalem who put it on record in an article in the *International Herald Tribune* of 14 February 1972. He found a different version of the Josephus *Testimonium* in a tenth-century Arabic text, a *History of the World* written by Agapius, bishop of Hierapolis in Syria. Agapius quoted the *Testimonium*, but without those Christian turns of phrase that had aroused so much suspicion. Professor Pines commented that it is scarcely believable that a Christian bishop would have watered down the original Josephus text or cut out any phraseology flattering to Jesus. If he has indeed discovered the original text of Josephus's *Testimonium* (and references to it by other ancient writers would suggest that he has) we have here the oldest non-Christian written evidence concerning Jesus.

Here is the Josephus passage, as quoted by Agapius, in the version held in the Hebrew University of Jerusalem:

'At that time there lived a wise man called Jesus. His conduct was good and he was held in esteem for his virtue. Many people, Jews and others, became his disciples. Pilate condemned him to death by crucifixion. But those who had become his disciples did not abandon his teaching. They declared that he had appeared to them three days after his crucifixion and that he was alive. Perhaps he was the Messiah about whom the prophets said so many wonderful things.'

Many people consider the evidence of the ancient Jewish sources to be decisive. These fulminate against Jesus, often trying to discredit him and his mother as well. But in so doing they certainly do not deny his existence; they confirm it. Klausner, a Jewish scholar who has examined the Judaic documents on Jesus, has remarked that 'they do not in any way impugn the historicity of the gospels; they merely use them as material for their scorn and reproach'.

Much the same can be said of the pagan opponents of early Christianity: not one of them supplements the usual defamatory accusations with doubts as to the historical existence of the founder of the new cult.

The ancient evidence taken as a whole can leave us intellectually certain that Jesus did exist. That the official pagan historians paid him scant attention is hardly surprising; their concern was with mighty kings and great sages. Jesus left behind him no magnificent palaces, no temples, no coins bearing his name and profile, no insignia of battle and conquest.

He left behind him only something intangible, something apparently unimportant: his message, entrusted to a group of rough provincials.

It is no accident that the ancient documents say less about his existence than about the 'political' effects his existence produced. The historians passed Jesus by; but they did pay attention to Christianity, which was taking the form of an organised, lively and disturbing 'cell' that could not be broken up or 'dispersed'.

The cross; inexplicable as an invention

A quick glance, finally, at how absurd it is to suppose that any myth would have been embodied in the utterly 'unsuitable' protagonist of the gospels.

We have already noted the commonness of his name, the lack of renown attaching to Nazareth, the lack of references to his education, the ordinariness of his carpenter's trade, the lack of references to his physical appearance, as well as other considerations that would have made this a myth completely unique in world mythology.

Somebody once remarked that to imagine converting the pagan ancient world by floating the idea of a Jew as Saviour would be like trying to convert a nineteenth-century Frenchman to the religious cults of the Congo – such was the disdain in which all things Jewish were held.

But there is one other absurdity – that of death on the cross. Of all the many deaths possible, why choose to give your mythical hero the death that the ancient world most despised?

Historical evidence that the cross was no mythical invention is provided by the fact that for the first few centuries (so long as the cross remained in use for executing the worst criminals) Christians were so ashamed of the way their God had died that they refrained from depicting his death in any visible shape or form. For the first three centuries the symbol of Christianity was not the cross itself: the cross was referred to only indirectly, by means of symbols such as a ship's mast with a transverse bar, an anchor, a snake twined round a plant, a plough, a man praying with arms outstretched. ...

The oldest drawing of the crucifixion dates from the third century; it was found in 1856 on the Palatine Hill in Rome. But it is the work of a mocking pagan, for nailed to the cross there is an ass.

The cross at Herculaneum to which we referred earlier, though acknowledged to be an authentic trace, is the one and only – so far as is known. A number of experts consider that its curtain or screen (of which traces were found on the nails) was there to cover it not so much because it was prohibited but rather because it seemed shaming to the faithful.

If, then, the early Christians took centuries to reconcile themselves to the thought that their God had met his death by crucifixion, how is it possible to suppose that those very same Christians invented, in their 'myth', this particular form of death? If all was legend, why did they not choose a less repulsive way of embodying the myth of a God who was to suffer death? Stoning, for example, as in Stephen's case; or beheading, as with John the Baptist.

It is up to those who defend the 'invention' theory to come

up with some answers – answers based on history, not ideology. Questioning is pointless if the only answers it evokes are ideological presuppositions.

Guitton was not, we feel, mistaken when he wrote:

'No matter from what angle you approach the problem, if you make what is recounted about Jesus arise out of faith in Jesus – thus making him the end-product instead of the initial element and the motive force – you make the origin of Christian worship and preaching incomprehensible.'

And it was Guitton (who spent a lifetime pondering these problems and watching the critics shift about from one position to another searching vainly for a sure foothold) who remarked that 'if criticism leads you away from the historicity of Jesus, criticism of criticism can lead you back again'.

9.

Where do you come from?

When Pilate heard them say this he became more afraid. He went back into the Praetorium and said to Jesus: "Where do you come from?" But Jesus did not answer him.

JOHN 19, 8–9

The continual violent anti-church propaganda typical of the modern age has always stopped short of attacking the person of Jesus, sensing that to insult him would be to insult oneself, one's own ideals, the desires of one's own heart.
Unlike any other glorious event or figure in history or poetry, the figure of Jesus has never been considered a fit subject for clever jokes.

BENEDETTO CROCE

A mystery that throws light

Any serious consideration of the New Testament requires one not only to attempt to solve the historical enigma constituted by the person of Jesus and his destiny; it also requires one to face up to the problem posed by a teaching, an ethic, which the passage of nearly twenty centuries has by no means rendered invalid. Indeed, there are grounds for saying that in Christ's vision of the world the sensibilities of modern man discern one steady point of reference amid the rise and decline of one ideology after another and the disappearance of so many ancient religions.

'Nothing of what this man said to the people in Palestine has lost any of its worth for people today. In the course of two thousand years many things once believed true have been proved false by the march of history, and the same fate will befall much that will be believed true in the year 2000; but his message remains true to itself, for all time and beyond time.'

In this chapter we shall try to see the justification for this apparently triumphalistic assertion by a contemporary French writer, Chabanis. As we saw at the end of the fourth chapter, the message which some people would have us believe attributable to backward communities of fanatics has been of immense relevance in the development of human history. But it has also been of unique universality, in both time and space.

The problems a Christian has to tackle as he reflects on his faith are numberless and daunting, wrote Cardinal Newman one day. But, he added, they are all in the end solved by the sure conviction that a God like this one and a message like this one cannot possibly have been invented.

This mystery of Jesus does indeed seem to be the *mystery which throws light.* A mystery which, as Pascal remarked, seems humanly inconceivable; but without this mystery man is more incomprehensible than ever.

Continuity in time

Concerning *universality in time.*

The simple, apparently elementary, verses of the gospels have nourished the great medieval and baroque theological 'summae' of Catholicism as well as the austere theologies of the Reformation and the far-seeing interpretations of the Eastern Orthodox. They have sustained the asceticism of the great mystics as well as the unwearying activity of the outstanding propagators of the Gospel; the immense diversity of the Church's saints is striking evidence of the fecundity of the gospel message.

Many of these verses have slaked the thirst for justice of atheists and anti-clericals who, in their struggles for a new and better world, have seen in Jesus not an enemy but a travelling companion and a source of inspiration.

The churches have used the Gospel as a tool with which to construct their theologies and institutions. But this very same Gospel has also been grasped by rebels, honest men and utopia-builders of all times as a fearsome weapon with which to denounce hypocrisy, knavery and betrayal on the part of those who were serving not Jesus but themselves. Not for nothing did the ecclesiastical powers-that-be at times discourage the reading of these four little books, restricting and even forbidding their dissemination.

In a quite extraordinary way Jesus and his teaching have survived even when belief in God has faded away. Many modern trends of thought claiming to be 'Christian atheism' advocate retaining – as the unsurpassed norm of wisdom – the ethical model attributed to Jesus while denying it any religious significance.

We have already drawn attention to the phenomenon whereby every age interprets Jesus and the gospels according to its own ideology, philosophy and culture. It is a phenomenon which, although adversely affecting the scientific reliability of much research, nonetheless testifies to the exceptional richness of a teaching that each generation can read afresh in the light of its own experience.

Continuity in space

Universality in space. Of all the 'religious' messages there have been, this is the only one which has proved in the course of history that its validity is not restricted to any one group, any one society, any one civilisation. Christianity is not Judaism – a religious phenomenon bound up with one particular race; it is not Islam – a faith that has never established itself for any length of time beyond the tropical zones; it is not Hinduism – the product of a specific culture of the Indian sub-continent; it is neither Confucianism nor Buddhism – expressions of highly individualised oriental cultures; it is not Shintoism – the distillation of Japanese national traditions.

The gospel message is the only one that has been able to take root and thrive throughout the centuries from the poles to the equator. Even the divisions among Christians, while on the one hand they do believers no credit, on the other hand do provide evidence that the Gospel has such a rich potential that it can take on many different shapes and forms.

By its endurance and expansion the message of Jesus has passed the 'test of history' that Gamaliel set it one day in the Jewish Sanhedrin: "*Leave these men alone and set them free; because if this enterprise, this movement is of human origin it will break up of its own accord, but if it comes from God you will not be able to destroy them*" (Acts 5).

A textbook for living

We have neither the space nor the competence necessary for a detailed look at the psychological value of Jesus's teaching as it has been discovered by present-day experts in the human sciences.

One psychoanalyst has said of the gospels: 'While I am reading them I am at the same time being read.' His words bear out what is said in the second chapter of John's gospel: 'Jesus never needed to be told anything about man, for he himself knew what was in man.'

More than a few have declared that the ethic proposed in the gospels constitutes a therapy which, psychologically, is admirably suited to the full development of the human personality. Or to the recovery of a balanced personality. In other words any human being, believer or sceptic, could use the gospels as a reliable textbook for living.

If that is so, it is another proof of what is affirmed by believers: that the Christian revelation throws light not only on the mystery of God but also on the mystery of man.

Pascal: 'For a religion to be true, it has to know human

nature. It has to know human nature's strengths and weaknesses, and the reasons for those strengths and weaknesses. What religion knows human nature as Christianity knows it?'

These are delicate and complex problems about which we can say only very little in the next few paragraphs. One thing however is certain: theories which would exclude the transcendental from the origin of Christianity must reckon not only with the discoveries made by archaeology and exegesis but also with the progress registered by the human sciences.

A secular ethic

Sigmund Freud was once asked to sum up his 'prescription' for defending man from the undefined evils that arise from deep within him. '*Lieben und arbeiten*', 'loving and working', was the answer of the founder of psychoanalysis.

Oddly enough it is the New Testament formula: love and work are central to the gospel message, although the second aspect is less well known than the first in spite of Paul's reminder to the Thessalonians in his second letter to them: '*We gave you a rule when we were with you: not to let anyone have any food if he refuses to do any work.*'

We need not dwell on the present-day preoccupation with loving. According to the gospels, Jesus regarded those who fail to show love as 'sinners' – wrongdoers not so much because they 'give offence' to some abstract deity but rather because they go against the profound needs of their own nature and thus injure themselves. They break the commandment '*You are not to kill*' because they kill in themselves all possibility of growth – of 'hominisation', to use the term dear to Teilhard de Chardin.

'*He who loves his brother abides in the light*', but '*if you refuse to love you must remain dead*' warns John in his first letter. This biblical terminology signifies the radical choice between becoming truly human or leading a life devoid of meaning.

In this sense the ethic attributed to Jesus and developed in the New Testament letters is a profoundly secular one. It is not meant exclusively for a group of believers; it is proposed for the consideration of all – to be used as an aid in avoiding attitudes that run counter to one's own true nature. It is a morality which could not be more different from the other 'religious' ethics, with all their 'purity' rules, their pettifogging legalism, their meaningless taboos and privileges that put a man in chains in the name of some presumed 'glory of God'. It is an ethic for the ordinary man, who need not necessarily be a 'religious' man.

It is no accident that, from the very beginning, Jesus's message has been called a Gospel, a piece of 'good news'. In other words it is not a series of *requirements* imposed by God (as in every other religion) but a series of *gifts* bestowed by God.

The message of radical love

Attempts to play down the novelty and psychological richness of the gospel teaching – by claiming that the precept of love is common to other religions – have no objective justification. Christianity has been put in a class all by itself by modern scholars who have devoted much effort to study of the phenomenon of religion, Van der Leeuw and K. J. Saunders in particular. The latter's classification is based on the reply a religion gives to the question: 'What ideal of man is proposed as the subject for imitation?' For Greek mythology it is the handsome and virtuous man; for ancient Rome and the Japanese Shintoists it is the disciplined warrior; for the Jews the 'just', righteous man; for followers of Confucius the 'kingly' man; for Hindus the ascetic; for Muslims the man completely submissive to Allah the all-powerful. Only for Christians is the human ideal the 'saint', that is to say the man who shows love.

In point of fact the originality of Christian teaching lies

not simply in the precept of love but also in the completely new concept of love for one's enemies – a concept never arrived at by Judaism or Islam, the other two monotheistic religions.

In the Old Testament those who were to be loved by the righteous and 'just' man did not include enemies, or even foreigners. 'Love your neighbour' meant 'Love those of your own race'. So the words of Jesus recorded in Matthew sounded radically new: "*You have heard it said: You shall love your neighbour and hate your enemy. But I say to you: Love your enemies and pray for those who persecute you, so that you may be the children of your heavenly Father; for he makes the sun shine and the rain fall on the just and the unjust alike.*"

A few unwary scholars have asserted that the Christian ethic derives from the *Manual of Justice* of the Qumran Essenes – which is considered to contain some of the most elevated moral teaching in pre-Christian Judaism. But this *Manual* says: 'Let the brethren love all the sons of light and let them hate all the sons of darkness.' Among the 'sons of darkness' were practically all those who were considered to be outside the small circle of the most strict Jewish observance. So it is pure illusion to think that at Qumran there was any suggestion of loving one's enemies.

Hell for some believers

The teaching attributed to Jesus is yet again unique in the emphasis it places on practice in contradistinction to theory. It is not adherence to a creed that brings salvation: people who have never heard of Christ can enter 'the kingdom of God'. It is one's behaviour that counts. "*Not everyone who says to me: 'Lord, Lord ... !' will enter the kingdom of heaven, but those who do the will of my Father who is in heaven.*" In other words, those who put their love into practice.

In another passage in Matthew this completely new point of view is clearly spelt out; devoid of all religiosity, it can be seen to be valid for all without distinction. On the day of judgment many will be amazed on hearing themselves called '*to take for your heritage the kingdom prepared for you since the foundation of the world*'. To those among them who murmur that they have never so much as heard of him, Jesus will reply that they have won the right to enter because they have overcome their selfishness and shown active practical concern for others; they have given him food when he was hungry, drink when he was thirsty, lodging when he was a stranger, clothed him when he was naked, visited him when he was sick or in prison. And to those who ask, more amazed than ever: "*Lord, when did we ever see you in those conditions?*" he will answer: "*I tell you solemnly, whatever you did for one of my brethren, even the least of them, you did for me.*"

Thus it is not necessary to profess a particular creed and call Jesus 'Lord' in order to live in harmony with this morality. All that is necessary is to demonstrate one's humanity by showing active practical concern for others. Conversely, it is not enough to believe that Jesus speaks in God's name, and as God himself, in order to have right of entry into the promised Kingdom. Indeed it is said that among the first to enter the Kingdom will be many whom the 'believers' have thought 'lost', forever 'outside' because they haven't recited any morning or evening prayers, haven't attended Mass, have often sworn and even blasphemed. ... But they have shown their love in practice. Whereas it is by no means certain that all 'believers' will succeed in gaining right of entry.

Once again some of the critics should explain why, if the believing community were responsible for this doctrine, they attributed teaching of this type to Jesus – teaching that drives a coach and horses right through the exclusiveness and dogmatism typical of any religion that is trying to establish itself, and of Judaism in particular.

These criteria for judging men are contained in the gospel of Matthew, the one directed towards the Jews with their ingrained sense of professing 'the one true religion'; for whom it was necessary not only to believe in Yahweh the one true God but also to carry out punctiliously any number of specific practices and refrain absolutely from any number of others.

Surely such praise of 'anonymous Christians', such an assertion that the kind of love that will ensure salvation is not found only among Christians, is a positive hindrance to missionary activity. It really does seem illogical to suppose that the early communities of believers elaborated this teaching themselves. The simplest, as well as the most logical, explanation does seem to be that the gospel-writers were *obliged* to put on record doctrine that was not of their own devising; for it is too discomfiting, and even self-defeating, to have been the product of a Church intent on mission.

Mario Pomiglio has aptly remarked: 'Sometimes the evangelists appear not to have understood what had been said, but they do not venture to alter the wording. ... I think this is unique in the history of literature: usually an author is in control of his characters, shaping them and forming them so as to convey through them, as mere channels of communication, his own thought. But in the case of the gospels it is Jesus who is in control of the writers; and they, as unassuming listeners, are intent only on preserving what he in fact did say.'

Christ the outsider

Nothing about the behaviour of the man described in the gospels fits in with the 'models' and 'types' isolated by our modern sociologists. Many of his attitudes were 'deviant' in the context of the society from which he sprang and which might have been expected to 'condition' him.

According to the evangelists, even Pilate the worldly sceptic ("*What is truth?*") was troubled to the point of being frightened by this mysterious outsider who so amazed him. "*Where do you come from?*" he asked, letting his uneasiness become apparent. He was more than nonplussed.

The character described in the gospels also fails to conform to what our sociologists call 'the behaviour required by the role'. One of the roles Jesus was expected to fill was that of an 'ascetic'. Every Jewish prophet used to give proof of his credentials as a 'man of God' by the austerity of his habits. Little has changed since then, for society still usually expects its religious models to display asceticism.

But a reproach frequently levelled at Jesus was that he had no qualms about 'eating and drinking', even in doubtful company. John the Baptist had done the decent thing by living on locusts in the desert like any self-respecting prophet; but this man Jesus was always making an exhibition of himself – '*a glutton and a wine-bibber*'. ...[1]

Perhaps the most scandalous of the eating and drinking episodes was the one recounted by Luke (chapter 7). '*One of the Pharisees invited him to a meal. When he arrived at the house and had taken his place at table, a woman of ill-repute in the town came in.*' Obviously a prostitute. '*She bent down behind him at his feet and began to weep; her tears bathed his feet, and she dried them with her hair; then she covered his feet with kisses and anointed them with the sweet-smelling ointment*' she had brought with her in an alabaster jar. Consternation all round. But the outraged host got none of the expected reaction from Jesus, only a reproof for himself; whereas the woman got from him a caring response: '*Your faith has saved you; go in peace.*' No doubt the Pharisee had expected a 'man of God' to depart in high dudgeon, 'contaminated' by the touch of so sinful a woman.

There is no trace in the gospels of any attempt to gloss over the character traits that made Jesus so unlikely a

Messiah. Even the most 'spiritual' of the four, that of John, tells us that the first of the 'signs' by which '*Jesus manifested his glory*' so that '*his disciples believed in him*' was the miracle at the wedding-feast at Cana. The least conventional, from a strictly religious standpoint, of all possible miracles. For what was the motivation? Nothing but worldly enjoyment. More to drink. And better drink too. ... Does this look in the least like a text devised by religious fervour? What a debut for a mythical religious hero.

"*When you fast, perfume your hair*"

We have already noted the difference between the Essene and the evangelical concepts of love; later we shall see other radical qualitative differences between these two preachings, which both emerged from the same national culture at much the same point in history. For the moment let us simply remark that one of the Essenes' rules was: 'Let nobody dare to use perfumes on the sabbath.' Josephus, who knew them well from having spent several years among them, said that 'they look like children beaten down by their master's cane'.

By contrast, for the believer in the 'good news' there is to be no outward display of 'mortification of the flesh'; no gloom, no long faces. "*When you fast, do not put on a dismal look as the hypocrites do: they disfigure themselves to show men that they are fasting. ... But when you fast, perfume your head with oil and wash your face, so that your fasting may not be apparent to men but to your Father who sees all that is done in secret.*"

One of the most remarkable characteristics of the ethic attributed to Jesus is its synthesis – not encountered anywhere else in the history of religion – of 'body and spirit',[2] 'nature and grace', 'sorrow and joy'. There is a time for feasting and a time for fasting. But even the latter must not put paid to rejoicing. Above all it must make no concessions to the sort of behaviour that makes one recognisably 'a religious type'. For that is precisely what Jesus is recorded as having rejected.

The God of the gospels gladly accepts invitations to our parties, and he is no teetotaller; but at the same time he teaches us that in order to follow him we must deny ourselves and take up our cross daily.

He is a God who decrees feastings and junketings if a dissolute son who has squandered his all on women returns home repentant. And he chides severely the 'respectable' son who protests, not unreasonably, that this is 'not fair'.

What 'priest' of no matter what religion (not excluding a certain type of sociological Christianity) would not throw up his hands in horror and declare in favour of the son who had stayed at home and worked? What Jewish religious community would have dreamed up, as an example of its ethic, a father who seemed to abdicate all parental rights? Ancient Israel's principles governing the upbringing of children are well expressed in, among others, the book of Ecclesiasticus (Sirach), chapter 30: '*He who loves his son will whip him often. ... Pamper a child and he will frighten you; play with him and he will cause you grief. ... Give him no freedom in his youth, and do not shut your eyes to his shortcomings. ...*'

So here too the character in the New Testament shows himself to be a moralist who turned all the hitherto immutable conventions upside down. The impossibility of explaining Jesus by situating him in some ideological framework becomes ever more evident.

Death and the family

If we examine his attitudes to *death, the family, women and children*, we can see more clearly still the extent of his departure from the religious traditions that are alleged to have made him up out of nothing.

First, death and the family. In four short verses at the end of the ninth chapter of Luke we seem him putting freedom and the message of love way ahead of customary funeral rites and family ties.

'*To another he said: "Follow me." But the man said: "Lord, let me first go and bury my father." He said to him: "Leave the dead to bury their own dead: for your part, go and proclaim the kingdom of God." Another said: "I will follow you, Lord; but first let me take my leave of my household." Jesus answered him: "No one who puts his hand to the plough and looks back is fit for the kingdom of God".*'

In the Old Testament, in chapter 19 of the first book of Kings, the prophet Elijah called Elisha to follow him in his mission: '*Elijah passed close to him and cast his mantle upon him. And he left the oxen and ran after Elijah saying: "Let me kiss my father and my mother and then I will follow you." And he said to him: "Go, and then come back ...".*'

So not even Elijah, one of the greatest of the prophets, the one whom the Jews expected to return just before the coming of the messianic era, felt able to stand in the way of filial devotion. Yet that is what the Christ of the gospels is made to do.

Much else in Jesus's treatment of family affection does violence to Jewish feelings in the matter:

Luke, chapter 14: "*If anyone comes to me and does not hate father and mother and wife and children and brothers and sisters, and even his own life, he cannot be my disciple.*"

Matthew, chapter 10: "*He who loves father or mother more than me is not worthy of me; and he who loves son or daughter more than me is not worthy of me.*"

Matthew, chapter 12: '*While he was still speaking to the crowd his mother and his brethren stood outside asking to speak to him. But to the man who told him he said: "Who is my mother and who are my brethren?" And stretching out his hand towards his disciples he said: "Here are my mother and my brethren".*'

And again in chapter 10 of Matthew, the ultimate in outrage: "*For I have come to set a son against his father, and a daughter against her mother, and a daughter-in-law against her mother-in-law; and a man's enemies will be members of his own household.*"

It is generally agreed that Jesus's attitude towards family ties, his refusal to regard them as sacrosanct, was absolutely unique in the context of contemporary society whether Jewish or pagan. How *did* Engels manage to define his doctrine as 'a mixture of middle eastern theology, particularly the Judaic, and Greek philosophy, particularly the stoic'?

Women

While death and the family cease to be regarded as sacrosanct, women and children – at that time generally little esteemed – have their worth enhanced.

Although Judaism recognised in principle the equality of the sexes (the first chapter of Genesis says: '*God created man in his own image, in the image of God he created him; male and female he created them*') in practice it emerged as 'a man's religion.'

One old Jewish prayer read: "Blessed are you, Lord, who have made me not a woman." While the husband boldly addressed God in these proud words the wife would resignedly murmur: "Blessed be the Lord who has made me according to his will." In some passages in the Old Testament the woman is listed as part of the patrimony at the disposal of the male (father or husband). In Ecclesiasticus, chapter 42, '*Better is the wickedness of a man than a woman who does good*'; and in the book of Proverbs women are 'stupid', 'quarrelsome', 'fickle and fanciful'.

Even today a different Semitic society, that of Islam, has still not progressed far beyond that.

But the rest of the ancient world treated its women even more deplorably, in some instances denying that they were human at all and attributing to them only an animal nature. The cult of Mithras, the ancient Persian light-god, which vied with Christianity until the fourth century, excluded women completely; if they wanted a religion they could turn to the cult of Isis – or else to ritual prostitution. ...

Nor were the great pagan sages much better. Socrates passed women over in silence; Plato held that except for sexual pleasure (though young males were preferable) there was no place for them in any well-organised society. Epictetus, the stoic thinker, put them on the same plane as the pleasures of the palate. For Euripides, woman is 'the worst of all evils'; for Aulus Gellius 'a necessary evil'. For Aristotle she is 'by nature defective and incomplete'; for Pythagoras woman was created 'from the bad principle that also generated chaos and darkness' whereas man came 'from the good principle that generated order and light'. Cicero's view was that if only there had been no women, 'men could have held converse with the gods'.

It scarcely needs to be said that the eighteenth-century Enlightenment and nineteenth-century Positivism did little for women. But it is worth noting that even today no lodge of Freemasons, even in France, accepts women as members.

But to return to the person whom the gospel-writers call Jesus.

He is shown as having reserved for women the privilege of the first of his resurrection appearances – as if to throw down an open challenge to all ancient cultures. Some of his best teaching is addressed to women, and ex-prostitutes are to be found among his followers. At times he is made to look almost like a man 'kept' by women '*who had been cured of evil spirits*' and from whom '*seven devils had been driven out*'; women with pasts that have always aroused the scorn of the censorious. But is it not to his credit that he did not scorn contact with these outcasts of society – these shocking examples of the lesser breed?

He sent away 'in peace' the adulterous woman whom the bigots wanted to see stoned. A few of the Fathers of the Church found this episode in John's eighth chapter so scandalous that they preferred to consider it an 'interpolation'. But the early Church had apparently felt itself obliged to record it.

John's gospel also describes the risen Jesus entrusting Mary Magdalen with perhaps the most solemn of all missions: "*Do not cling to me because I have not yet ascended to the Father. But go to the brethren and tell them: I am ascending to my Father and your Father, to my God and your God.*" Yet one of the greatest of ancient Israel's teachers, Rabbi Eliezer, wrote: 'Better to burn every word of the Law than entrust it to a woman.'

There are other examples – the Canaanite woman in chapter 15 of Matthew, and the wise virgins in chapter 25 – of Jesus's recognition of women's faith and constancy. Perhaps the most outstanding of all, the one that shows his total disregard of the traditional role of the woman, is the one in the tenth chapter of Luke:

'*As they went on their way he entered a certain village. A woman named Martha welcomed him into her house. She had a sister called Mary, who sat at the Lord's feet and listened to his teaching. But Martha bustled about doing the serving; she went to him and said: "Lord, do you not care that my sister has left me to do all the serving by myself? Won't you tell her to help me?" But the Lord answered her, "Martha, Martha, you fret and get anxious doing too many things. Yet few are needed; indeed only one: Mary has chosen the better part and it is not to be taken from her*".'

Not only does Jesus not accept that the woman's role is invariably and exclusively domestic; he goes as far as saying that for women too 'the better part' is that of doing 'the one thing necessary' – that is to say seeking the truth, listening to the message of salvation.

In Jesus's view the difference between the sexes is incidental and transitory, entailing no essential difference between the male and the female. Both roles are destined to disappear: "*For in the resurrection they neither marry nor are given in marriage, but all are like the angels of God in heaven*" was his answer to some Sadducees who asked him a catch question concerning marital status. Husband and wife, son and daughter, male and female – all these he saw as 'images' in a world that was destined for transformation; they certainly did not point to a division into two of the human race, which is one and indivisible. 'God created mankind in his own image'; he created mankind 'male and female', but for this present life only.

The gospels tend to replace the distinction between men and women by a distinction between the married and the celibate – regardless of sex. Here too there is a rejection of cultures that cruelly despised unmarried or barren women on the grounds that they were 'failures' in the one and only relationship with men that seemed to count in antiquity. Women are not obliged to become wives and mothers in order to fulfil their mission in life as human beings.

Those who pour scorn on what they are pleased to call 'the sexophobe myth of the virginity of Mary' perhaps fail to recognise the message of liberation it conveys. The gospels show us not only that the Messiah was 'born of woman' (thus giving the woman, all women, the dignity of 'mother of God') but also that that particular woman was a virgin (after as well as before the birth, Catholic faith insists) and had not 'known a man'; yet she was not on that account to be accursed (as official custom would have had it). On the contrary: "All generations shall call me blessed."

Children

In the civilisations of antiquity the child was considered incomplete as a person. Infanticide was in some cases officially decreed; in no case was it considered on a par with homicide. In Rome and at Athens the child had no right to life until after the ceremony of 'recognition of paternity'; the father was thus free to decide to kill the child if he so chose. Plato maintained that it was necessary to leave children of very poor families to die; Aristotle asserted that the bringing-up of lame children ought to be forbidden by law.

Within Judaism, the Essenes totally excluded children, just as they excluded old men.

But of Jesus we are told that he refused to chase children away when they came running towards him; not only that, but he roundly rebuked those disciples who tried to do so themselves. Moreover in a complete reversal of the values normal at the time, in Jewish society particularly, he went so far as to praise them as exemplars: "*Unless you become like little children you cannot enter the kingdom of God … for the kingdom of God belongs to such as these.*" According to the book of Proverbs (which is attributed to Solomon) children are stupid and in need of the rod: childhood is a sort of illness, curable with time and chastisement. But Jesus declared to his disciples that children have a very special relationship with God: those who dare to maltreat them should therefore beware. One of his outbursts of anger was caused by the thought of anyone harming them: "*Better for that man to have a millstone tied around his neck and be flung into the depths of the sea.*"

A *'successful form of Essenism'?*

Discovery of the Qumran manuscripts dashed the hopes of those who thought the explanation of many puzzling aspects of the Christian message lay in the Essenes. Previously the sect was known about only because of a few references to it by classical authors and by Josephus, so it was easy for Renan to dismiss Christianity as nothing but 'a successful form of Essenism'.

But he might have done well to note that, unlike the early Christians, the Essenes were never persecuted by the Jewish religious authorities. On the contrary they were considered models of piety, which is a clear indication that their spirituality intensified the strictness of Judaic observance and certainly did not run counter to it.

We have already seen how Jesus's teaching differed from that of Qumran where children, penance and love of one's neighbour are concerned. The *Manual of Justice* lays down that: 'The stupid, the feeble-minded and the backward, the blind, maimed, lame, deaf and disabled – none of these can belong to the community'. Moreover sinners, foreigners and women are all to be kept at a distance. Exactly the opposite of what we see in the New Testament figure who makes a point of granting privileges to despised minorities, and enjoys sharing a meal with just the types of people from whom the Essenes fled in horror.

Sabbath observance was carried to quite ludicrous lengths at Qumran, so full of scruples were these 'holy men'. Again, exactly the opposite of Jesus who said "*The sabbath was made for man, not man for the sabbath*", thereby scandalising not only the Essenes but every Jew there was.

The *Manual of Justice* lists with the greatest possible precision many regulations affecting food and hygiene, all food being classed as either 'clean' or 'unclean'. Traces of this classification are still apparent in Judaism to this day.

But the Jesus of the gospels said: "*Listen to me and understand. Nothing apart from man that goes into a man can contaminate him: what comes out of a man is what contaminates man.*"

The Old Testament had laid down detailed rules and regulations governing the ritual cleansing and 'purification' of both persons and food. These rules (unlike others) did not originate in concern for hygiene or good manners: they show that the Jewish prophetic tradition had accepted the idea that only those who had made themselves 'clean' in a material sense too could have access to the 'sacred'. 'Uncleanness' restricted both persons and things to the realm of the 'profane'.

Jesus's assertion that the things of this world are never

impure in themselves but are rendered impure only by the thoughts and reactions of men seems to many scholars one of the most puzzlingly unprecedented elements of his teaching. Not only does it show a Jew challenging the authority of Moses himself; it calls in question all the liturgical ritual of the ancient world with its expiatory and sacrificial customs.

The Essenes increased both the number and the complexity of the Jewish 'purification' regulations. This alone shows how wide was the gulf between the teaching of Qumran and that of the gospels.

The Master of Qumran decreed that his teaching was not to be imparted to the 'unholy': the Essene wisdom was to be kept secret so as to isolate the sect as far as possible from 'sinners and the unclean'.

But Jesus on the other hand said: "*Does anyone bring a lamp and then cover it with a sack or a screen? It is to be set on a stand so as to give light. Indeed there is nothing hidden that will not be made manifest, nothing secret that will not be brought to light.*"

His preaching and his work were not intended as a rallying-cry to the 'just' and the devout; nor was it his purpose to establish a 'faithful remnant'.

The Essenes preached a form of dualism by which humanity was divided into 'sons of light' and 'sons of darkness'. For Jesus there was no *a priori* division between the good and the bad: all *ought* to repent because all *can* repent.

Humility and service

The doctrine the gospels attribute to Jesus suggests that political power and glory are a major evil. He is recorded as saying that 'the kingdoms of the earth' are entrusted to Satan who distributes them to those who worship him, the devil. He seems almost to recommend social abasement when he remarks that "*he who humbles himself will be exalted and he who exalts himself will be humbled*'. In his eyes the blessed – the fortunate – are the meek, the humble, the peacemakers. Not those who battle for a place in the sun.

He thus introduces a value that was quite unknown to the cultures of antiquity – humility. Classical Latin had no word to express it: *humilis* had a pejorative meaning and was applied to anything 'base', 'ignoble', 'of little worth'. Only after the coming of Christianity did the word take on a positive moral meaning.

For the New Testament, life is a radical commitment to the service of others, a caring for others.

For humanity's sake

The fact is that the four little books called gospels propound a doctrine – of equality, respect for mankind, and universal salvation – more radical than any in history before or since.

The absolute equality of all, regardless of no matter what artificial classification, derives from the fact that all have the same father – the Father whom Jesus felt free to call 'Abba' – and are therefore all brothers and sisters.

Not only that. Although, as the gospels assert, Jesus and God are one, Jesus is also man; thus man and God are one. In the person of Jesus God and mankind are fused. The things of men become the things of God, and vice versa.

No other religion, and no philosophy, has ever come to the aid of man so completely and irrevocably. The humanism inherent in the Gospel can be underrated only at one's peril.

So long as God was thought of as a creator spirit, immutable and inaccessible as he dwelt in infinite space, it was all too easy to despise humanity. Man was at most God's 'creature', not God's 'son'; and the one could in no way be identified with the other.

If God alone is the perfection of being, there is nothing to stop man, that most imperfect creature, from being trampled underfoot. But if God has become incarnate – if God was born into the world and became a child, if he took his chance along the highways and byways like any other human being – then man cannot be insulted without God himself being insulted too.

H. Gollwitzer, a considerable authority on the relationship between Jewish–Christian messianism and the 'secular' messianisms of our day, has written:

'To declare that, for man, man himself is the supreme being is no guarantee against the exploitation of some by others if this declaration is made in the context of a theory that sees in man as we know him today only a preliminary to the man of the future, 'true man'. The messianism of man-made ideologies legitimises violation of the rights of present-day man. What must be made clear is that man today is not our property, to be manipulated for our own ends; nor is he the property of society, or of the great shapers of society. Man's humanity is safe and inviolable only when he belongs to a Master who is beyond our reach.'

The so-called 'myth' of the God of Abraham and of Jesus, the God who '*calls all of us by our own names*', can protect us from the danger of being used as materials for the construction of some society of the future, one designed by the philosophical, sociological and political speculation of other men.

Biblical 'obscurantism'

Jesus is recorded as having taught people to pray saying 'Our Father'. Not 'My Father'. That is an ever-valid response to all forms of racism and exaggerated nationalism.

"*From one single stock God created the whole race of men so that they might occupy the whole earth*" said Paul in Athens to some stoic and epicurean philosophers who argued with him (Acts, chapter 17). And Peter, according to chapter 10 of the same book, came to understand "*that God does not have favourites, but that anybody who fears God and acts justly is acceptable to him*".

The radical rejection of all racism stems from the universal paternity of God, in which all share equally.

Those who believe that if man is to be 'liberated' he must do away with the so-called 'obscurantism' of the Bible would do well to remember that the biblical tradition they so underrate, with its 'myths' about the one Father of all and of Adam the progenitor of all, is a defence for mankind against the insanities of racism. Adam, in scripture, symbolises men's innate equality.

The Enlightenment, the eighteenth century 'Age of Reason', set out to destroy 'the Adam myth'; in so doing it paved the way for the Nazi holocaust. It was thanks to Voltaire's 'Ecrasez l'infâme!' that millions were sacrificed to the racial gods of the Aryan myth.

Behind every system of thought that departs from the Judeo–Christian tradition, racism lies in wait. Greek philosophy saw the distinction between free men and slaves as 'a fact of nature'. Plato thanked the gods that he was born 'a man and not a woman; a free man and not a slave'. Aristotle devised his social system on the presupposition that 'barbarians' were born to slavery in chains.

Voltaire, having got rid of the Bible, naturally became a racist. Thirty of the 118 articles in his *Dictionnaire Philosophique* hurl insults at the Jews whom he calls 'our bosses and our enemies, whom we detest and consider the most abominable people on earth'. Other articles in that Dictionnaire beloved of so many 'enlightened secularists' inveigh against the blacks, who are described as 'slaves of other men by nature'. Voltaire even rehashed the ancient Greek contention that non-whites were the product of mating between women and apes.

So long as the churches maintained their links with the Bible and its 'myths' of the one Father of all and Adam the progenitor of all, Christian anti-Semitism – shameful though it was – never went to the lengths of racism. The Jews were to be converted, by force if necessary, but in this they were no different from any other human beings; they were never to be suppressed because they were 'inferior', sub-human.

It was when Christian theology became most seriously polluted by Graeco–Latin thought, with its ambiguous God of the philosophers and its Aristotelian metaphysic, that little sprigs of racism appeared. This occurred especially in the sixteenth century, the Age of Discovery when theologians disputed whether the inhabitants of the Americas were men at all and whether, therefore, they had such a thing as a soul. The Dominican Bartolomeo de Las Casas, the 'Indians' saint', promptly reminded the hellenised theologians of the great Judeo–Christian message: '*Our Father*'.

Notes

1 According to Mark Jesus not only enjoyed his wine but also knew something about wine-making: "*Nobody puts new wine into old skins; for the wine would split the skins and both wine and skins would be spoilt. New wine has to go into new skins.*" And Luke suggests that he had a palate: "*Nobody who has drunk a mature wine is interested in the latest vintage; he says the old is better.*" The contrast with John the Baptist is evident in the matter of dress too. John wore a rough garment of camel-skin, with a leather belt around his waist; Jesus had a fine tunic, woven in one piece from top to bottom – so good that the soldiers who crucified him finally drew lots for it, to save it from getting torn in the scramble to grab it.

2 The narrow-minded moralist is as far removed from the message of Jesus as the 'libertine'. Neither in fact has any respect for the body. And Christianity is essentially a belief in the resurrection of the body. According to Roger Garaudy, that resurrection has 'a very special value' for the Marxist; for it makes a sort of 'materialism' central to the Christian message, and detaches that message from the spiritual disembodiment typical of the 'religious' view of things.

10.

A misunderstanding?

Let all the nations gather together and all the peoples assemble: Which of them can declare these things? Let them produce their witnesses and prove themselves right, or else let them listen and say: "It is true".

ISAIAH 43, 9

'If Renan is right, God does not exist'

In the last chapter of Jean Guitton's admirable book *Jésus* there is a page well worth careful consideration:

'Claudel once said that when his sister Camille had made him read *La Vie de Jésus*, he had no hesitation in concluding: "If Renan is right, God does not exist."

'Indeed, if God – to be understood as perfection – exists, and if Jesus is a misunderstanding to which men have fallen prey, then that Supreme Being – understood as true, respectful of his creation, sovereign educator of man's conscience, head of the human family – has to be seen as a cruel ironist. The ultimate secret of the divine morality turns out to be sadism. God has played a malicious joke on the "privileged" human race, leading it to regard as the bearer of revelation, and even as a divine personage, that ambiguous, barely existent being called Jesus on whom, like ravens swooping on a corpse, all the ills of spirit and soul converged.

'And this misunderstanding was not confined to one small group of Jews in one short period of their history. For twenty centuries since then it has been misleading percipient, sensitive, wise and noble natures the world over.

'And the irony reaches third degree intensity. For that universal error and that bogus divine revelation have been far more beneficial to mankind than any knowledge of real forces and true causes. The misunderstanding which Jesus gave rise to has in its turn given rise to man's most glorious achievements: in the west it has been the regenerative driving force within history.

'But argument along such lines leads nowhere. One may as well go straight to the point and say: if Jesus does not exist, that is because God does not exist.'

But, Guitton goes on, despite all the familiar arguments in favour of the non-existence of a God of perfection, a God of love (above all the fact of suffering of all kinds present in the world), surely it is possible to see the question in reverse:

'If one leaves the existence of God altogether in doubt and tackles the question at the other end – that is to say if one starts from the fact of Jesus (refraining from dismissing it at the outset on the presupposition that God does not exist), and if one concedes that a number of different lines of experience converge in support of the fact of Jesus, then one may reasonably ask how – if not through the workings of a benevolent Providence – it is possible to explain the insertion into history of this unlikely figure.'

And then:

'If God is bound up with Jesus (in the sense that denying God's existence amounts to rendering the problem of Jesus void of all significance), then it can be said that, conversely, making the Jesus of the gospels a real person and not a myth amounts to restoring the probability of God's existence.'

The problem of evil

Only if God did manifest himself in the man Jesus does God's existence remain probable.

Only the omnipotent God who is said to have made

himself visible and tangible in Jesus can escape condemnation on account of the scandal of evil.

Jacques Natanson:

'The classic objection tries to place theism in a dilemma: either God is able to prevent evil and does not do so, therefore *he is not good*; or else God cannot prevent evil and therefore *he is not all-powerful.* In either case God lacks one essential attribute: goodness or omnipotence. And this entitles the objector to deny that he exists.'

Only if Jesus is the 'image' of God can the intolerable scandal that evil undoubtedly is become transformed into a mystery – the mystery of an Omnipotence which manifests itself to its creatures in the form of a crucified slave.

Only the God who manifested himself in Jesus, an innocent who was crucified like a slave, can escape being cursed by man for the waves of pain and suffering that so often engulf him.

Natanson:

'There is no reply to the problem of evil except the cross of Jesus, on which God underwent the supreme evil; and triumphed over that evil because he endured it to the very end. This reply certainly eliminates the obstacle of a tyrannical God who is supposed to view the sufferings of his creatures with complacency; but it also gives rise to an even greater obstacle to understanding.'

The God of Christ comes to our aid not through his omnipotence but through his weakness.

St Paul's first letter to the Corinthians:

'*The language of the cross is folly to those who are perishing, but to us who are being saved it is the power of God. ... While the Jews demand signs and the Greeks seek wisdom, we preach Christ crucified: an insuperable obstacle to Jews and folly to Gentiles; but to those who are called, be they Jews or Greeks, Christ is the power of God and the wisdom of God; because the foolishness of God is wiser than men and the weakness of God is stronger than men.*'

Just as Christianity is alone in not running away from the problem posed by a God who chooses to remain 'hidden', so too Christianity is alone in refusing to sidestep the problem of evil, placing it instead at the very heart of its message.

As was said in one of the closing messages of Vatican II – the one addressed to the poor, the sick and the suffering – 'Christ did not do away with suffering. He did not even wish to unveil to us entirely the mystery of suffering. He took suffering upon himself, and this is enough to make you understand all its value. ... You are the brothers of the suffering Christ; and with him – if you wish – you are saving the world.'

In the perspectives of other religions the sufferer can well believe that his God is abandoning him. In the perspective of the New Testament the believer who is oppressed by evil can be certain that his God, who has known tribulation, is closer to him than ever. 'Only the God who suffers is powerful enough to come to our aid', wrote Bonhöffer.

Face to face with the present day

Only if God did indeed manifest himself in the man Jesus does God's existence remain probable.

Not merely because only Christianity teaches that suffering can be redemptive but also because Christianity is the only 'way to God' that can stand up to modern criticism and present-day sensitivity. It is no accident that Christianity is the only religion to have produced that branch of theology known as 'apologetics', which sets out to demonstrate the rational and historical basis of the faith.

'The intellect', says one of the documents of Vatican II, 'is the friend of the Christian faith'.

It is certainly not our wish to decry the non-Christian religions. One cannot but be impressed by Buddhism's intense longing for salvation and its self-abandonment to the Eternal, by Hinduism's struggle for union with the divine through asceticism and meditation, by Taoism's disinterested love and self-immersion in the incomprehensible, by Islam's faith values.

And yet one is surely justified in being puzzled by the sort of ecumenism which goes far beyond emphasising the need for mutual respect and love and tries to minimise the radical novelty of the Christian message. In its essentials Christianity has very little indeed in common with the bric-a-brac of so much that goes by the name of 'religion'. Even where the monotheistic religions are concerned, we are convinced that 'monotheism is *not* the shared base on which are founded substantially identical religions that differ from one another only in respect of certain rites and customs' (Natanson).

We are convinced that Christianity is 'different', that the God it proclaims is indeed 'the absolutely Other'.

We believe that the words and actions of Jesus are always completely different from those expected of a God devised by men. This particular God, as Luther pointed out, has taken upon himself all the characteristics that men of every age have considered the precise opposite of divine: *humanitas, infirmitas, stultitia, ignominia, mors, humilitas.* ...

The God of Jesus is radically different from all human conceptions of divinity. Not for nothing is it declared that in order to know him man needed a revelation.

Mutual respect and brotherhood have nothing to do with the facile (and dishonest) ecumenism which says that 'after all, we all believe in God'. Yes, but which God?

When the day of reckoning comes

We can't help wondering what will happen when scientific criticism, comparable in aggressiveness to that levelled in the west against Christianity, sets about attacking the non-Christian religions.

Christianity – and we say this without triumphalism or even complacency – has weathered the storm. Its historical basis, far from crumbling, seems often to have been reinforced by scientific criticism. Its message, far from losing validity, seems to have been invigorated by present-day sensitivity.

But what will happen to the old and respected religious systems of Asia and Africa when they have to face up to the same trial by fire, at the hands not only of scholars but also of the people as a whole?

In Japan, China and parts of India, and some Islamic countries the day of reckoning has already arrived. Religious messages which for thousands of years had united peoples, given birth to wisdoms, moulded art and literature, are crumbling – often without any attempt being made to shore them up. And they are crumbling without having been subjected to any of the sledge-hammer attacks mounted by the west against the foundations of Christianity – in the name of 'science and reason'.

The Afro–Asian religious jungle is being flattened by the winds of change – by the spread of a universal culture, by the spirit of criticism and by political ideology.

Self-criticism in Japan

In an attempt to save something (tradition, ancestor-worship ...) from the wreck, a dismal form of self-criticism has come to the fore in Japan.

In 1945 the national religion, Shinto, was obliged to declare officially that the reigning dynasty was not of divine origin; that the emperor was not descended from Amaterasu the sun-goddess; that the eight Japanese islands were not 'born' from matings between male and female divinities.

The cult of the emperor and his image was abolished by decree. Thanks to American pressure, Shinto found the strength to undergo a very necessary surgical operation – amputation of its religious dimension that had ceased to be viable.

But it was the high degree of literacy in Japan (the

Japanese population is perhaps the most highly educated in the world) that forced Shinto to abandon its claim to 'sacredness' and declare itself henceforth 'pure Shinto' – in other words, nothing but a civil institution that has no purpose beyond preserving the old rites, the country's traditions and loyalty to the sovereign.

The empty sky over China

In China the three great philosophico-religious systems (Confucianism, Taoism and Buddhism) which for thousands of years had vied with one another for supremacy are now all suffering the same wretched fate. The first large-scale contact with the west in the middle of the last century had faced them with a crisis, but the fall of the Celestial Emperor signalled the beginning of their disintegration.

The two typical expressions of the Chinese spirit and its 'universism' (Confucianism and Taoism) had never achieved any appreciable spread beyond the frontiers of their own country. But now, in the People's Republic of China itself, Lao-Tse, Buddha and Confucius and all their philosophico-religious systems are consigned to the history-books.

They no longer seem to have any hold on the people, although from time to time the régime, in a burst of nationalistic pride, chooses to 'rehabilitate' one or another aspect of them. Which looks like proof that they are considered innocuous. ...

No news like that which comes out of the USSR (where 15% of city-dwellers and 30% of the rural population are said still to belong to the Orthodox Church after more than half a century of official atheism) comes out of the great Chinese People's Republic. In China Marxism seems to have put to flight once and for all the old gods that once peopled the sky for 650 million human beings.

The fragile pantheon of India

The government of India has a plan for salvaging the great temples of Hinduism, the religion claimed by 85% of the population. They are to be safeguarded at public expense, not as religious centres but as works of art.

There are very few real believers left; in many areas 'Hinduism is reduced to a pitiful state. One must not conceal the fact that in a sudden revolution Hinduism could crumble' (A. C. Bouquet).

Although a few *gurus* travel around Europe preaching Siva, Kali and Vishnu, Bouquet (one of the best-known and most impartial historians of comparative religion) remarks that:

'Notwithstanding all the efforts to present it as an essentially universal religion, Hinduism operates within a field no less restricted than that of Judaism. Undoubtedly it contains a few basic ideas that could easily be transplanted into any country in the world. But from an institutional point of view it is, like Nazism, strictly bound up with race and descent and is reserved for those who belong to some specific caste. Once one has been admitted to this rigid hierarchy, one is free to believe or disbelieve anything one chooses: idolatry, gross superstition and non-theistic philosophy live side by side with highly devotional theism.'

The overlapping of legendary beliefs, the proliferation of gods and the superimposed philosophies are all such as to make it almost impossible to state the exact content of this religion.

But it is when it encounters the spirit of *homo faber*, the man who wants to change the world, that Hinduism (like all the other non-Judeo-Christian religious systems) comes up against difficulties that seem insuperable.

For the faithful Hindu, the world is nothing but deceptive appearances. So the religious ideal becomes negation of the world and of life. A fatalistic attitude naturally ensues: if the world is only apparent and not real, there is nothing to spur one on to work towards improving it. The doctrine of the transmigration of souls maintains a rigid division into castes which, although abolished by law, still flourishes in half a million Indian villages.

The various Hinduisms seem incapable of any response to man's belief in the possibility of building a world in which a better life is attainable and justice is more widespread. So, as Bouquet remarks, 'there is an attempt to react by introducing into Hinduism as much Christianity as possible. Men like Gandhi have devoted themselves to service of their neighbour; but this was done at the expense of the theory, which had to be modified in order to admit of such an attitude.'

Doctrines of hopelessness

The plain fact is that Jewish–Christian belief sees the world as a reality, one that is good, created by a God who is separate from it and who created it of his own free will. '*God saw all that he had made, and behold it was very good.*' The words '*And God saw that it was good*' recur like a refrain throughout the Genesis account of creation.

So the Christian struggle against 'the world' is a struggle against certain ways of life among men in the world, and certainly not against the world in essence.

By contrast, according to the Asiatic religions – Buddhism first and foremost – the world's reality is nothing but an illusion that has to be dispelled and overcome. The ideal is not 'being' but 'non-being'.

In Christianity the fundamental aspiration is towards the transformation of the world and of reality, the attainment in the course of history of the 'Kingdom of God'. And in this sense the gospel message is profoundly revolutionary.

But in the Asiatic religions the fundamental aspiration is not towards the transformation of reality but towards escape from it; not a challenge to the world but a flight from it. 'No belief in renewal in the course of history, no impulse towards a transformation of society can derive from Nirvana, the Buddhist's ideal. The Buddhist views history with indifference, whereas the Christian takes it seriously.' Thus Paul Tillich, who sees a world of difference between the message of the Bible and the religious messages of Asia, which he tends to classify as 'doctrines of hopelessness'.

Faced with Mohammed

From a Christian point of view, Islam is a painful mystery of history. It is a thorn in the flesh for many apologists.

The religion preached by Mohammed is in fact the only great monotheism to emerge subsequent to the preaching contained in the gospels (although historically speaking the teaching of Islam is nothing but a mixture of Judaism and Christianity as they were known in Arabia at the beginning of the seventh century).

In the course of a few generations the Muslims – with a power of expansion similar to that of the Christians – swept away many of the most glorious of the churches: those of Egypt and the whole of North Africa, famous for producing saints and popes and fathers of the Church; those founded by St Paul in the Middle East; those of Persia. Even Jesus's own land was invaded and Mohammedanised. Islam then came to a halt, stabilised around the tropical regions, with a few outposts in the north in the Balkans. Yet it has since spread southwards in Africa and eastwards in Asia, and has always been resistant to every effort on the part of Christian missionaries. Wherever the two faiths have come in contact with one another they have been in confrontation, without either giving way at all significantly.

History is now treating the two somewhat differently. 'Islam', remarks Bouquet, 'is showing itself extremely vulnerable when faced with the spirit of the present day'.

'Ever since black Africa entered the modern era, Islam has fallen prey to a real crisis: it can be proved statistically that the degree of Mohammedanisation of a country is in inverse relation to the development of education in that country' (W. Bühlmann).

Even in its traditional areas Mohammedanism seems to be erecting defences around itself, closing the doors to the winds of change and trusting in the power of the secular arm. Thus in many Muslim countries the laws of the Koran are the laws of the state. The police will arrest any citizen found eating or smoking during the hours prescribed for fasting during Ramadan; anyone seen drinking a glass of beer or wine is liable to imprisonment – worse in the case of spirits – for the religious ban on alcoholic drinks is codified by the government. The sale of certain 'unclean' foods is forbidden by law; and television transmissions have to submit to strict censorship based on the Koranic prohibitions.

There is no Mohammedan state that is 'secular' in the present-day sense.

What will happen to Islam when the crutches it is borrowing from the police and the magistrature are taken away from it?

Bouquet: 'I do not dare to think what effect an "aggiornamento" could have on the doctrine of the Koran.'

What will be left of the Koran when criticism's razor is free to tackle that rich growth of poetry and religious feeling that is shot through with unresolvable inconsistencies and completely obsolete rules drawn up for desert nomads?

What will happen when not only the specialists but also the Muslim in the street become aware how much stratification, transcription and infiltration (from Judaic texts and the apocryphal gospels) the Koran has undergone – the Koran which Mohammedanism declares was dictated 'word for word' by God himself?

One Muslim theologian has remarked that Islam is now faced with the same problems that faced Christianity after the seventeenth century. It is in fact on the point of being subjected to attack 'in the name of reason'.

What will happen when widespread literacy, the modern critical spirit and present-day sensitivities confront Mohammedanism, in which 'man is held prisoner by a doctrine that does not recognise God as Father'? (Dutch Catechism).

We have already noted that the word *islam* means 'submission' and that the Muslim is 'the one who submits'. The ideal believer is therefore the *abd*, the slave, the personification of submission to a God separated from man by an unbridgeable gulf. 'Allah is inaccessible' says the Mohammedan profession of faith. Man is to love God out of sheer obedience; there is no question of communion of wills. The divine will is completely arbitrary. This really does look like a God who is defenceless against attacks mounted against him on account of the problem of evil.

What will the modern insistence on justice have to say to the Koran's failure to abolish slavery? Or to the humiliating roles it allots to women within the institution of polygamy?

What will present-day man's urge to transform the world have to say to the Koran's negation of autonomy to every being on earth? Everything is dependent on Allah, whose control of all things is direct and completely arbitrary: 'If tomorrow Allah wishes otherwise, things will be otherwise.'

This type of self-abandonment on the part of the believer leads to fatalism; for it is impossible to better one's lot if Allah has granted autonomy neither to things nor to men.

'*There is no other name under heaven given among men*'

Chapter 4 of the Acts of the Apostles tells of the arrest of Peter and John by the Jewish authorities, '*annoyed because they were teaching the people and proclaiming in Jesus the resurrection of the dead*'. Hauled before the Sanhedrin Peter, '*filled with the Holy Spirit*', went on proclaiming Jesus, asserting that '*there is salvation in no one else, for there is no other name under heaven given among men by which we are to be saved*'.

For those who believe in the one who said '*He who exalts himself will be humbled*' there can be no question of 'glorying' in the faith if that means enhancing its prestige by denigrating other religions. The whole of the New Testament speaks of a Saviour by whom we have been chosen, not one we have chosen ourselves; he is a gift to us, not an achievement of our own. Furthermore the Gospel shows us that his power lies in his weakness, his victory in the failure of the cross, his hope in men who were cowards.

On the other hand the Church makes no apology for wanting all men to know Jesus Christ and follow him. Or for her attitude to other religions, which cannot be other than that of a witness pointing to the one Lord Jesus as Lord of all men.

That is why Christianity will never capitulate to any 'syncretism', to any attempts to bring together in one all the religions of the world. No proposals for a 'natural' or 'universal' religion, no matter how seductive, will ever convince the Christian, who does not trust the high-flown, supposedly religious 'faiths' devised by man's reason or fancy but accepts a revelation which he sees as unique, unrepeatable and offered as a free gift.

The basic Asian dogma that every religion is a way to the deity, that all religions are of equal value and that therefore there is no genuine opposition between them, falls on deaf ears when it reaches those who accept the One who uncompromisingly said that he had come 'to bring not peace but the sword' and to be 'a sign of contradiction'.

Just as the Church has always taken care to refute those who assert that all religions are equally false, so too she has to refute those who assert that all are equally true. Thus the Secretary of the Vatican Secretariat for Non-Christian Religions was quite right to refuse to put his signature to a document, proposed to him at New Delhi in 1972, which would have committed the Catholic Church to work for the elimination of differences between religions. The God of the

Bible said "*I am a jealous God*". And in Isaiah, chapter 43: "*Before me no god was formed, nor shall there be any after me. I, I am the Lord, and apart from me there is no saviour.*"

The fact is that Christianity is not just one province in the vast empire of religion. It may look like that to an external observer. But Christianity knows itself to be not simply one of many religions but the all-sufficing and definitive revelation of God within history. At the heart of the faith there is, prior to any 'religion', the good news about Jesus, who came not to add something to humanity's religious inheritance but to reconcile the world to himself and thus to God.

All the same we believe with Paul Tillich that Christianity's problems today, and above all in the future, lie not so much in the encounter with the traditional religions (which are faced with so many difficulties that their long-term survival seems doubtful) as in the encounter with the secular religions, which are no less replete with dogma and cult practices – nationalism in its extreme fascist forms, liberalism in its extreme laicist forms, socialism in its extreme Stalinist forms – and with so many other 'religions' created by that inexhaustible fabricator of myths and fabulous gods, the heart of man.

The sort of atheism that strives to set men's hearts and minds free from gods of that sort ought not to be controverted by Christians.

But the sort of atheism that accuses Christianity of 'alienating' man does need to be brought to see that the Gospel shows God himself suffering alienation for the sake of man. '*God so loved the world that he gave his only Son*' and delivered him into the hands of men, leaving them free not only to kill him but also to bear witness to him throughout history – thus perpetuating his humiliation.

The God of Jesus shows himself to be not 'the One who is all in all to himself' who requires men to expend themselves in his service to the point of dehumanisation or 'alienation'.

He is the One who does not shut himself up inside himself but transforms himself – 'alienates himself' in fact: he is the Creator who appeared among his creatures in the form of a servant. And the only God who set out, himself, in search of men.

'He took the form of a servant'

To the God who manifested himself in Jesus the Church of the earliest years sang a hymn quoted by Paul in the second chapter of his letter to the Philippians.

This hymn, this kerygmatic fragment, is perhaps the key to the New Testament.

It is an extraordinary text, the exact opposite of so much religious alienation.

Here, in point of fact, the Church of the Apostles proclaimed the alienation of God himself:

'*Your frame of mind should be that of Christ Jesus:*

His state was divine
yet he did not cling
to his equality with God
but emptied himself
taking the form of a servant
and becoming as men are;
and being as all men are,
he became humbler still,
obedient even to death,
death on a cross.
For this God highly exalted him
and bestowed on him the name
which is above all other names
that at the name of Jesus every knee should bow
in the heavens, on earth and in the underworld
and every tongue should confess
that Jesus Christ is the Lord
to the glory of God the Father.'

If even this Jesus who is God is a 'misunderstanding', if – in spite of all the evidence to the contrary – we are here faced with nothing but 'a projection skywards of man's need for some sort of religion', then the centuries-old cry of Richard of St Victor – "Lord, if we are mistaken, it is you who have deceived us" – more than ever rings true.